The Truth Behind the Black Lives Matter Movement

And the War on Police

Ron Martinelli, Ph.D.

Forensic Criminologist

Martinelli, Ron, Ph.D., CMI-V
The Truth Behind the Black Lives Matter Movement and the War on Police

Includes bibliographical references.
ISBN 978-1-944783-52-5

First Printing

Published in the United States by
Martinelli & Associates, Justice & Forensic Consultants, Inc.

Cover Design by Image Creators Design Studio, Austin, TX

Dr. Ron Martinelli's law enforcement and forensic site is found at
www.DrRonMartinelli.com

Contents

Foreword

It was an honor to have been asked to write the foreword for Dr. Ron Martinelli's book *The Truth Behind the Black Lives Matter Movement and the War on Police.* I have known Ron for a number of years. As police consultants, we worked cases together. And while I spend a great deal of time analyzing training issues and force policy, Ron devotes much of his time to the forensic aspect of police confrontations. I've read Ron's reports. I've watched him testify in court, and I know him to be a no-nonsense, "tell it like it is" police professional. And in this text, Ron does it again.

Beginning with the first chapter, Ron starts his treatise with the history of the Black Lives Matter (BLM) Movement. Nowhere in the mainstream media will you see a more complete amalgamation of how, and by whom, this radical, dangerous, anti-police organization was organized. These are names that most citizens, let alone most police officers, have never heard of. Yet as Ron explains, these individuals are admittedly bent on changing the conditions of what they call the "black oppression" of African-Americans through a systematic program of "police terrorism" and "police violence" by today's law enforcement officers. Here's a short summary of some of what you'll learn when you crack open this book.

- The real story of the *Trayvon Martin-George Zimmerman Incident.* Ron shatters the myth that the much-maligned State of Florida "stand your ground" provision was a factor in this incident.

- The forensic facts behind the *Michael Brown-Officer Darren Wilson* shooting, better known as the Ferguson Incident. Ron will take the reader on a minute-by-minute recap of this life-and-death confrontation between all 6'4" 292 pounds of the not-so-gentle giant Michael Brown and Officer Wilson. You'll read about the indisputable forensics that resulted in the clearing of Officer Wilson.

- The truth about the *Cambridge, MA Police Sergeant James Crowley-Dr. Henry Louis Gates Incident.* You'll learn how President Barack Obama, during his "police acted stupidly" press conference, initially stated he "did not know if race [was] a factor" in the incident but ended his comments with "this incident shows how race remains a factor," coupled with his declaration that "there's been a long history in this country of African-Americans being stopped disproportionately by police."

- What really happened between *Freddy Gray and the Baltimore MD Police Department?* A little known fact is that Gray, a known drug dealer with no less than fourteen priors in the preceding eight years, did indeed have in his possession a spring-assisted knife and had both cannabinoids and opium in his system – and exhibited behavior consistent with swallowing the drugs.

And throughout these well-known police confrontations, you'll find how the Black Lives Matter (BLM) Movement, famous for its gruesome and hateful chants of "Pigs in a blanket, fry 'em like bacon" and "What do we want? Dead cops. When do we want them? Now!" injected itself into each incident.

Ron destroys the myth shouted out to any media pundit who'll listen that "one black man is murdered by police every twenty-eight hours." Ron's research found that in reality, only one out of every 173,871 black males dies as a result of police force.

Ron also shoots down the blatant lie appearing in a popular Black Lives Matter (BLM) blog that "more than 1,000 people are killed each year by police." The BLM writer responsible for that canard compounds that lie with another dramatic made-up statistic: "nearly 60% were unarmed."

In Ron's text, you'll learn the truth about police use of force, especially the use of deadly force. And he'll analyze BLM's "10-point Campaign Zero" plan to repair the law enforcement and justice system, including their call for "ending the militarization of the police," a program that is already being implemented by President Obama by Executive Order and in essence dissolved the 1033 Program that allowed agencies across America to secure needed tactical equipment.

No less than 36 footnotes, 26 legal cites and 83 additional authoritative references are contained in this heavily annotated book. While Ron is an experienced police procedures expert who is used to giving opinions in court, you won't find a lot of them in this brief reference book. What you will find is a ton of important and relevant facts.

This book belongs in every police department library. In fact, in my opinion, it needs to become a part of all police academy curricula. In my nearly four decades of police work, I have never seen a more detailed or researched text on BLM, a well-organized, well-funded, radical, dangerous, national anti-police movement.

The Truth Behind the Black Lives Matter Movement and the War on Police is a well-written and easily readable text that will no doubt provoke a powerful and negative emotional response, as Ron takes an unflinching stand on the cultural, societal, and political factors that underlie the BLM movement. But, like it or hate it, it is a must read for every cop in America today. Every person who wears the uniform needs to know "the truth."

David M. Grossi

Law Enforcement Trainer and Consultant

Acknowledgements

Although I am the author of and the moving force behind this book, I readily admit that it would have taken much longer to produce without the assistance of a number of people who jointly contributed to its development and production. My wife Linda, who continues to provide excellent feedback and constructive criticism in the many research projects I undertake, provided the logistical support necessary for the eventual print and electronic publication of this book.

Members of my staff at Martinelli & Associates, Justice & Forensic Consultants, Inc. including my Administrative Assistant Shelby Gale, MFS, and my researcher analysts were instrumental in assisting me with gathering and vetting research reference sources from the various governmental, organizational, private, and media Internet and print sites. This was necessary for securing the statistics, data tracking and statements of the involved parties quoted in this book. It also allowed me to put some very complicated data, as well as organizational and socio-criminal issues, into context so they would be understandable for the lay reader.

For personal security purposes, they are not identified in this book. They know who they are and the debt of gratitude I owe them. Special thanks to our crime analyst Alexis Manning, MS, for providing and vetting the crime and death statistics used in this book.

I am truly fortunate and blessed to have a uniquely qualified forensic staff who work tirelessly in pursuit of our joint mission and motto "In Search of the Truth." I am also extremely grateful to my staff for always giving 110% to enhance our firm's positive reputation within the law enforcement, forensic, and criminal justice community where we provide, as we like to say, "Forensic solutions; not speculation."

This book was edited by linguist, speechwriter, communications expert, and English composition professor Alan Perlman, Ph.D., who worked tirelessly with me to fine-tune the manuscript.

Finally, I would like to personally thank all of the professionals and other individuals who agreed to be interviewed by me to provide additional context to remarks I have quoted from various reports, papers, articles and other news stories and social media posts. You all allowed me to remain objective instead of speculative in my presentation of materials and information.

Ron Martinelli, Ph.D., CMI-V, BCFT, CFA

Forensic Criminologist, Certified Medical Investigator,

Certified Force Analyst

Preface

I am a forensic criminologist, a Certified Medical Investigator, and a police practices expert who specializes in the forensic investigation and analysis of police related use of force and death cases; the investigation of domestic radical, militant, socio-political movements is certainly not something I and my staff are inclined to do for a living.

However, I have spent nearly my entire adult professional career either in government service as a law enforcement officer or as a forensic expert often tasked with the very challenging mission of speaking for others who cannot speak for themselves. Recently, this mission has led me to the examination of a broad movement that unites isolated police-related death cases into a perceived pattern and a false narrative with dire implications for our society and our democracy.

The investigation of death is what I am trained to do. In large part, the birth of the Black Lives Matter (BLM) movement commenced with the death of two young black men named Trayvon Martin and Michael Brown, who were tragically killed as a result of instigating violent confrontations with others. Now that the investigations and one criminal jury trial are concluded, the forensic facts that everyone in the BLM movement refuses to acknowledge are that both Martin and Brown were shot and killed by victims acting justifiably in self-defense. One victim was a civilian and the other, a police officer.

Having investigated and forensically analyzed what police practices experts refer to as the "totality of circumstances," of each shooting incident, I was both intrigued and disappointed that the race of the decedents took immediate political precedent over the obvious forensic facts of each circumstance. The blatant criminal acts of both Trayvon Martin and Michael Brown were ignored; the victim civilian and police officer shooters were vilified in the press and publicly by under-informed politicians and in one case a state prosecutor; false narratives were forwarded by "hashtag journalists"; and both shootings were investigated politically rather than forensically.

In good measure, the BLM movement, which was founded upon the false narrative of "Hands up; don't shoot," rose like a dangerous phoenix from the ash heap of burning black-owned businesses in Ferguson, MO, after the officer-involved and justifiable shooting of felon Michael Brown.

The law enforcement and criminal justice communities; federal, state and municipal governments; our minority communities; and all Americans should be very concerned about the Black Lives Matter movement, because it is not what it appears to be.

As I will explain later, in every city the BLM movement has visited, crime has risen exponentially and shows little indication of waning. The BLM movement and its members and supporters light the fuse that ignites a never ending cycle of violence and polarization between minorities and law enforcement/government, and that is a process that affects all Americans. I and other experienced members of the law enforcement and forensic community firmly believe that police officers have been deliberately targeted and assassinated in part because of the false and hateful messages spread by this movement.

This book peels back the layers of the BLM movement "onion" and exposes it for what it really is: an organized, well-funded, radical Marxist octopus of ancillary militant groups and organizations that seek to defund law enforcement that protects the rule of law, in order to overthrow our democratic way of life.

As you read on, you will learn how we forensically analyze the BLM movement through the systematic use of vetted research and intelligence gathering. You will find no emotional, heart-rending arguments here. This is an apolitical, non-speculative guide to a growing movement with disingenuous designs for all Americans. Whether you are a law enforcement administrator, a police officer, a member of the criminal justice or governmental communities, a member of the media, an educator, or simply a concerned citizen, this is a must-read book for your library.

Many in the law enforcement, criminal justice, social science, forensic and journalistic communities will view this book as a "go to" reference guide when researching and responding to statements, so-called facts and the rhetoric of the Black Lives Matter movement. However, others who belong to or otherwise support the movement will criticize the book and my findings as being controversial.

I fully anticipate being criticized by members of the BLM movement, their uninformed liberal supporters, black activists, and the liberal mainstream media that has done little to investigate the many false narratives of this militant movement. As a former police detective and a battle hardened forensic expert, I have never shied away from controversy. In fact, I welcome the opportunity to present the other side of the story and the forensic facts.

If you take away anything from this book, it should be that as Americans, we need to be vigilant and tenacious in pushing back those among us who attempt to diminish or dissolve our democracy by spreading falsehoods designed to create or enhance a toxic atmosphere of polarization between our various communities. As you will read in this book, the ultimate purpose of the BLM movement is to promote a radical and sometimes violent Marxist plan designed to tear apart the fabric of American society. As Americans, we cannot allow this to happen.

"All it takes for evil to exist is for good men to do nothing."

Edmond Burke

Full Disclosure

While you may conclude that this book is pro-law-enforcement, it is important to understand that as a forensic expert, my job and mission is to seek out the truth wherever it lies. Credible experts do not advocate for entities or persons; we advocate for objective facts and forensic evidence. Attorneys, politicians and activists advocate for people and entities.

As a Federal and State Courts qualified forensic criminologist, a Certified Medical Investigator, and police practices expert, I accept all manner of cases to investigate, analyze, and opine on - prosecutorial, criminal defense, civil agency/officer defense, civil rights plaintiff cases, and the occasional court appointment.

While slightly over 60% of my cases involve retentions by a state, municipality, law enforcement agency, or officer(s), my remaining practice comprises non-agency/officer clients. Of these, the vast majority are plaintiff cases involving allegations of serious abuses of civil rights and/or wrongful death at the hands of law enforcement. I have analyzed and opined in more civil rights cases on behalf of plaintiffs than many of the plaintiff's attorneys who have opposed me and am the prevailing expert in approximately 90% of my retained cases, no matter what side has retained me.

As I will explain later, as a forensic police expert, I have seen my share of frivolous civil rights litigation unfairly filed against officers who were merely doing their jobs under extreme and deadly circumstances. However, I have also investigated, analyzed, and opined in cases where officers committed severe abuses of civil rights; many of the victims were black and other minorities. Therefore, this book in no way discounts those well documented incidents.

This book is ultimately about objective, scientific facts and context. Credible context is something I have found to be sadly lacking throughout the Black Lives Matter movement. For example, BLM advocates seldom delve into the actual behavior that precipitated or compelled an officer to take forceful actions. The movement's rhetoric is replete with anti-law- enforcement, anti-government false narratives and Black Nationalist racial hatred. The surrogates of the BLM movement consistently employ pseudo-science to forward their talking points.

Leaders of the BLM movement, the movement's supporters, black activists, and exploitative politicians seeking votes are complicit in spreading the false narratives of the movement. The BLM organization, as a whole, is a radical, revolutionary, political movement. Like expedient politicians, the leaders and surrogates of the movement have learned that if they simply repeat mistruths and self-serving "Hands up! Don't shoot!"-style slogans often enough, naïve and uninformed people within the black and minority communities will believe them. It is absolutely Hitleresque and dangerous.

To counter these strategies, I have tried to do the most thorough and painstaking job of researching and writing about what I, as a disinterested, impartial criminologist and police expert, have found to be the objective and scientific facts behind the allegations made by the leaders and supporters of the Black Lives Matter movement.

I have also provided you with a unique opportunity to look behind the curtain shrouding the movement, its co-founder leaders, its supporters, and its financiers. And I have listed all of the references I have used to write this book, along with websites so that you can become your own forensic investigator. Please don't take my word for what the BLM movement is all about. Begin your own journey to better educate and inform yourself and others as to the dangers of this radical, activist movement.

Martinelli & Associates, Justice & Forensic Consultants, Inc.

Martinelli & Associates, Inc. (est. 1980), is a forensic investigation, consulting and training firm based in California. The firm provides government agencies, courts, the legal community, and various municipal and corporate entities with forensic, legal support, and training delivery services. The firm has the nation's only multidisciplinary Forensic Death Investigations and Independent Review Team (FDIT), comprising experienced experts in homicide, law enforcement, forensics, medicine, and all forms of applied science, complete with laboratories. The firm's experts and FDIT are involved in many of the nation's high-profile police-involved death and civilian self-defense homicide cases.

Grammar note: I have decided, for the sake of simplicity, to use *he/his/him* to refer to indefinite persons or things, e.g., *A police officer must use his judgment.* Such usages are, of course, meant to apply to women as well.

Chapter 1

The Inspiration – Birth of a Movement

The Black Lives Matter (BLM) movement was founded by Alicia Garza, Patrisse Cullors, and Opal Tometi in 2013, following the acquittal of George Zimmerman, a private citizen of mixed race, who shot and killed a 17-year-old black teen named Trayvon Martin in self-defense while being violently attacked in a condominium neighborhood in Sanford, Florida. The movement gained significant steam following the officer-involved fatal shooting of 18-year-old Michael Brown by Officer Darren Wilson in Ferguson, MO on August 9, 2014.

Immediately after Zimmerman's acquittal, San Francisco-based Garza, an organizer with the minority labor unions' advocacy group National Domestic Worker's Alliance, took to social media through her Facebook page and presented to her black followers the proposition that "Black Lives Matter." Garza's stirring appeal was subsequently taken up by her friend and colleague Patrisse Cullors, a self-described "Freedom Fighter," who founded the jail/prison inmate advocacy organization Dignity and Power Now in Los Angeles. Black activist and social media savvy Opal Tometi, who directs the pro-immigration advocacy organization Black Alliance for Just Immigration (BAJI), joined Garcia and Cullors with her Internet plea to "end the disproportionate arrests, imprisonment and killing of black Americans by police."

BLM co-founders Garza, Cullors and Tometi describe their Black Lives Matter organization on its website as a "chapter-based national organization working for the validity of black life; and working to rebuild the Black Liberation Movement." According to the BLM's founding statement, the movement is rooted in the experiences of American blacks who actively resist their "dehumanization." [1]

The BLM's founders state that their movement is an "ideological and political intervention where black lives are systematically and intentionally targeted for demise." Their foundational statements include, but are not limited to, assertions that blacks are deprived of basic rights and human dignities; they are the victims of "systematic extrajudicial killings and genocide" at the hands of law enforcement and vigilantes; and they "bear the burden of state-sponsored Darwinian experiments that attempt to squeeze [them] into boxes of normality defined by white supremacist state violence." The BLM's founding documents are replete with references to and language advocating for "unlawfully arrested black political prisoners" and undocumented illegal aliens.

Furthermore, the BLM's founders maintain that blacks are universally seen as irrelevant and without value in a white supremacist society that inflicts a disproportionate level of state-sponsored violence upon them. The movement's founders espouse a paranoid message to blacks, accusing "white society" of creating a system that impoverishes, controls, and unlawfully surveils blacks. They accuse white society of "hyper-criminalizing and sexualizing black people and [their] allies." The three BLM founders state that their BLM movement "remains in active solidarity with all oppressed peoples who are fighting for their liberation and know that their mutual destinies are intertwined."[2]

As you'll see in Chapter 4, the BLM movement's founders lean heavily upon Marxist ideology. The language used throughout the founders' writings and their media interviews is that of "oppressed peoples" engaged in a Marxist-style revolution seeking liberation from a "white

---

[1] Black Lives Matter website, www.Blacklivesmatter.com

[2] Ibid., Black Lives Matter website, www.Blacklivesmatter.com

supremacist" society whom they have clearly identified as their oppressors.

As will be explained and well documented throughout this book, the BLM movement is far from a sporadic, disorganized, haphazard, flash-in-the-pan, social protest mob. This is an organized, well-funded, media-savvy, national and international movement, based upon revolutionary Marxist ideology. The movement seeks to systematically attack, diminish, and eventually overthrow the rule of law and the democratic form of government to free whom they see to be the oppressed masses.

Chapter 2

How it all began: George Zimmerman Shoots Trayvon Martin - the scientific facts

One of the most infamous, yet misreported, misstated, and misunderstood shooting incidents of this decade has been the self-defense shooting homicide of Trayvon Martin, 17, by private citizen George Zimmerman, 28, in Sanford, FL on February 26, 2012. Although Zimmerman was ultimately acquitted on July 13, 2013 by a jury who reviewed all of the evidence of the shooting and killing of Martin, the verdict was not embraced by a mostly uninformed public. George Zimmerman has also not helped his cause following the verdict by being involved in questionable incidents in his personal relationships.

For the most part, the mainstream media's reporting of the alleged circumstances of the encounter between the Neighborhood Watch Captain Zimmerman and his assailant Trayvon Martin was an excellent example of media bias and "hashtag journalism." Rather than presenting a truthful account of the forensic facts and evidence, most of the mainstream media and their reporters had long since made up their minds as to George Zimmerman's culpability in Martin's death.

Generally speaking, the media and many in the public could not wrap their minds around why and how an armed adult could shoot and kill an "unarmed" black teenager. This apparently included Black Lives Matter movement founders Alicia Garza, Patrisse Cullors and Opal Tometi. The killing of Martin by Zimmerman, who was initially described as being Caucasian, outraged the women and planted a seed. The subsequent acquittal by a jury of Zimmerman in Martin's death resulted in the actual birth of the Black Lives Matter movement.

Many of us, including myself, could point to George Zimmerman's lack of prudence in the manner in which he initially followed Trayvon Martin around the Sanford condominium complex on the night of the shooting. However, the actual circumstances and forensic facts of the encounter between Martin and Zimmerman; Martin's deliberate encounter with and violent assault upon Zimmerman; and Zimmerman's self-defense shooting/killing of Martin need to be forensically explained once and for all.

Here are the facts and evidence behind this controversial shooting. Some of it has never been reported in the mainstream media. In a couple of instances, the State Prosecutor successfully (and I believe unethically) motioned to keep the Zimmerman jury from reviewing this important and relevant evidence.

Many might agree that George Zimmerman lacked good judgment on the evening of the incident. Some might even go so far as to accuse him of being stupid, myopically focused on neighborhood security, and perhaps even a "wannabe cop." However, that is far different from being a "murderer," which he was not.

I am confident that many of you will find this presentation of facts and evidence both illuminating and contextually relevant in the determination of Zimmerman's guilt or innocence in the murder of Trayvon Martin.

The Prosecution's "Search for the Truth." Really?

An investigation is a "search for the truth." The only "advocacy" for an investigator and a prosecutor should not be for any person or entity, but for the facts and forensic evidence, as best as can be determined. As attorneys and forensic experts often say, any case "is what it is." Unfortunately, in the case of George Zimmerman's shooting of Trayvon Martin, the Florida State Prosecutor's Office turned what should have been a simple is-what-it-is forensic investigation into a political shooting, purely for racial expediency and political favor.

The re-branding of Trayvon Martin in preparation for trial

From the inception of the investigation and throughout the period of the Zimmerman trial, Trayvon Martin's family and his defense team were consistently engaged in damage control and the re-branding of the teen as an innocent victim. But Martin's background, demeanor, and behaviors were far from angelic.

In reality, Trayvon Martin's look, stature, and persona at the time he confronted and assaulted George Zimmerman were far from the Photoshopped image of the 12-year-old, innocent-faced, hoodie-wearing kid who was consistently portrayed in countless media stories and on posters carried by protesters during the trial. It is the image still maintained by Black Lives Matter demonstrators today.

The photos on Trayvon Martin's former Facebook site depicted a much older, physically larger and a more menacing person. During the course of the Zimmerman investigation and trial, Martin was consistently referred to by his family, their civil attorneys, and race baiters such as Al Sharpton and Jesse Jackson as a "child." In reality, Martin's autopsy report indicates that he was lean and muscular at approximately six feet in height and weighing in at 158 pounds. This was in comparison to George Zimmerman's weight at the time he was arrested: his booking report documents his stature at a short and chubby 5'7", weighing 194 pounds.

Trayvon Martin's family, perhaps under advice from their civil attorneys, took down the minor's Facebook and Twitter pages immediately following the shooting. I was lucky to capture some of the photos and texts from these sites before they were abruptly removed. These sites featured damaging photos and "tweets" of Trayvon Martin growing marijuana, throwing up gang hand-signs, talking about his desire to obtain a gun, holding a gun, and openly bragging about "gangstas" and "ass kickings."

In Martin's Twitter account were text messages inquiring how he could obtain codeine he needed to make the popular, dangerous, and highly addictive street drug called "Lean," a concoction of Arizona Iced Tea,

Skittles candy and codeine-based dextromethorphan (DXM) cough syrup. If you recall, the naïve and uninformed media repeatedly reported that Trayvon was just "buying candy" before the shooting incident, when CCTV surveillance footage showed him at a local store innocently purchasing a can of Arizona Iced Tea and a package of Skittles.

This was not some innocent kid just buying candy. There is little doubt what the teen had in mind that night. Two of the psychological presentations of a person who consistently drinks "Lean" or other DXM/codeine-laced street drugs are paranoia and aggression. You do not even need to be under the influence of the drug or have it in your system to display these symptoms if you have a history of taking Lean. Did these presentations have anything to do with Martin ultimately accosting and beating George Zimmerman immediately before his death? Food for thought.

Trayvon Martin's Facebook and Twitter friends who posted on his sites consistently referred to him using the term "cuzz," the Crips street gang term for a fellow gang member. Martin's Twitter account clearly showed that Martin, who went by the street moniker "Slimm," was involved in drug activity and in concocting the dangerous and highly addictive Lean. His Facebook moniker was "No Limit Nigga," not exactly an innocuous pseudonym for a young black male.

State prosecutors and trial Judge Nelson were well aware of Martin's postings on Facebook and Twitter. They were also aware that Martin's parents were divorced and that the teen had lived with his mother in the Miami-Dade, FL area, until she had abruptly sent him to live with his father in the condominium complex the day before his death because of his criminal behavior, a recent arrest, and his suspension from Dr. Michael Krop Senior High School.

The prosecutors and Judge Debra Nelson were aware that just before Martin's mother had moved him to Sanford, police had detained Trayvon and had found him to be in possession of a burglary tool and expensive women's jewelry that he could not account for. He had also been previously suspended from school for being in "an unauthorized area" on or near campus on one occasion and, on another, for graffiti vandalism and possession of a marijuana pipe and narcotics residue.

The circumstances of Martin's "trespass" are unclear, and his school records were inexplicably sealed by school officials after the shooting by request of his parents. Again, we see the theme of information blackout instead of transparency. Unfortunately, a sympathetic and complicit mainstream media neither questioned nor investigated Martin's past criminal behavior to determine whether his possession of burglary tools and stolen property might be connected with his suspicious activity in the condo complex when observed and followed by George Zimmerman.

Trayvon Martin was an at-risk youth in need of serious supervision. He was associating with the wrong people, engaged in criminal behavior, and assertively heading down the road marked "Caution – Trouble Ahead!" One would have to be a weak, busy, naïve, uninvolved, or absent parent to not intervene sooner.

Apparently, Trayvon's mother had finally had enough of the bad influences that the Miami-Dade area had on her son and wanted him out of there. That is why Trayvon suddenly appeared on the door step of his father's residence in the Twin Lakes Condominiums complex in Sanford, FL. Unfortunately, Trayvon's father neglected to inform the Twin Lakes Homeowners Association, as required, that his son was going to be living with him. Perhaps if he had, the HOA might have advised their appointed and entrusted Neighborhood Watch Captain George Zimmerman, and the incident might have been avoided.

Hiding the pea under the shell – the concealment of exculpatory evidence

The concealment of discovery evidence, especially evidence that might prove to be exculpatory to the defense, is referred to as a "Brady Violation" and may, in this case, have violated George Zimmerman's civil right of due process. The actions of the Florida state prosecutors might be considered unlawful and even a bar violation by competent legal experts.

In this case, the deliberate concealment of evidence gleaned from Trayvon Martin's cell phone conclusively showed that Martin's mother Sybrina Fulton and the teen's biological father Tracy Martin had lied to state investigators about the details surrounding Trayvon's nefarious and criminal activities before his fatal encounter with George Zimmerman.

Ben Kruidbos, who was the Florida State Attorney Office's IT director, was troubled about possible prosecutorial Brady violations. He was so concerned about his personal liability, because State Prosecutors Angela Corey and Bernie De La Rionda did not reveal evidence to Zimmerman's defense team that they had discovered, that he hired his own attorney for consultation after notifying his superiors and State Prosecutor Corey.

It is interesting to note that State Prosecutor Corey fired Mr. Kruidbos immediately after the conclusion of the Zimmerman trial. Following his termination, Kruidbos notified the State Prosecutor's Office of his intent to file a civil "whistleblower" lawsuit for wrongful termination against his former employer. In May of 2016, a Florida State Superior Court Judge ruled with "extreme prejudice" against the Florida State Prosecutor's Office and State Prosecutor Corey, allowing Mr. Kruidbos' civil suit to continue forward.[3][4]

Judge Debra Nelson, who presided over Zimmerman's trial, not only ignored the prosecutors' possible Brady violations, but granted the prosecution's motion to exclude all of the damaging evidence of

---

[3] http://theconservativetreehouse.com/2015/05/28/controversial-florida-state-attorney-angela-corey-loses-counterclaim-suit-against-zimmerman-witness-ben-kruidbos/

[4] http://www.freerepublic.com/focus/news/3050299/posts

Martin's background. It is apparent that the jurist considered Trayvon to be the "victim" in this incident.

Her Honor eventually did allow Zimmerman's defense team to finally view the information prosecutors had withheld. Judge Nelson informed the team that she had ruled against the presentation of any evidence damaging to Martin because she felt that the photos, text messages, and evidence about his past suspicious behavior and criminal history lacked relevance to the immediate circumstances of the shooting. However, Judge Nelson had no scruples about allowing the jury to hear all about Zimmerman's criminal justice education and about a martial arts class he briefly attended. Not exactly what one would consider a legal *quid pro quo*.

As a court qualified subject matter expert in self-defense homicide investigations, I could not disagree more with Judge Nelson's decision to exclude evidence of Trayvon Martin's recent police detention for possession of a pry tool that could be considered a "burglary tool" and possible stolen jewelry; his aggressive tendencies; and his questionable character.

This information would have been critical for a jury to consider because it spoke directly to the legal issue of George Zimmerman's "collective knowledge" as to what might have reasonably constituted suspicious and possibly burglary-related activity in a neighborhood plagued with similar crimes. As Zimmerman's defense team presented in court, Zimmerman, as the Twin Lakes HOA's Neighborhood Watch Captain, was keenly aware of suspicious behaviors that might be criminally related, and it was this activity which drew his focus to Trayvon Martin in the first place.

I had discovered and revealed in prior articles that in the year before the shooting incident (2011-12), there were over 400 calls for police service in the 206 units of the Twin Lakes condominium complex. Sanford Police Department officers who took the stand during the trial testified that Zimmerman's neighborhood was plagued with residential and auto burglaries.

At the time of the shooting, the City of Sanford, FL itself was no place for the faint-hearted. The city's crime rate was 22.6% *higher* than that of the state and 150% *higher* than that of the entire country. Indeed, Sanford's property crimes rate was a whopping 176% *higher* than Florida's, and the city burglary rate was an amazing 232% *higher* than for the US as a whole.

As the Twin Lakes' appointed and entrusted Neighborhood Watch Captain, George Zimmerman already knew all about the intense crime rates in and surrounding his neighborhood. Therefore, when he observed Trayvon Martin, whom he did not recognize as a resident, and Martin's presence in a darkened area behind a block of condo units, he was relying upon his collective knowledge of how burglars prowl prior to committing thefts.

It is irrelevant that Zimmerman did not know about Trayvon's past history because we know that he did not. However, it would have been important for his jury to be able to connect the dots between Martin's past criminal history of being in places from which he was restricted and his prior arrest for possession of a burglary tool and expensive women's jewelry for which he could not account. This knowledge would have allowed these "triers of fact" to understand Zimmerman's statements that his attention had focused upon Martin because he believed that the teen's actions and behavior were highly suspicious. Now you understand *why* it was so important for the state prosecutors to keep this information from the jury.

Racial profiling: who profiled whom?

There has been much discussion of George Zimmerman's alleged "racial profiling" of Trayvon Martin on the night of the shooting. While this might make for interesting social commentary, there was *never any credible evidence* that Zimmerman ever racially profiled the black teen. The jury members never believed this, and at least two jurors have said as much after the conclusion of the trial.

It is clear that Zimmerman did not racially profile Trayvon Martin as a black male. However, he did profile Martin's *activity* as being sufficiently suspicious to warrant closer scrutiny. The rule of law and the legal standards of proof care not what anyone "believes" with respect to the issue of criminal culpability. The standards include the presentation of credible circumstances, statements, facts, and irrefutable forensic evidence, combined with guilt beyond any reasonable doubt.

In the Zimmerman case, it was clear to the jury and those of us who investigate, analyze, and testify in homicide investigations that the Florida State Prosecutors came up way short on facts and forensic evidence that George was guilty of 2nd degree murder. Their presentation of so-called incriminating "evidence" was high on emotions and unsupported speculation - and short on actual facts and forensic evidence.

In actuality, the state prosecutors had known for months that they had no real evidence that Zimmerman racially profiled Trayvon Martin. However, this never stopped them from continually spreading this false narrative through their supportive media surrogates.

The only trial evidence of anyone racially profiling was in fact Trayvon Martin himself. Martin's former girlfriend and reluctant witness Rachael Jeantel testified in court that immediately before Trayvon's confrontation with Zimmerman, Martin had referred to Zimmerman during a cell phone conversation with Jeantel as "a creepy white cracker" who was following him.

The precipitating event that led to the shooting

One important forensic and evidentiary fact appeared to have weighed on the minds of the jurors: timing. Why it had taken Trayvon Martin at least thirty minutes to walk a distance of only less than a mile in the rain from the 7-11 store to the scene of the shooting off Retreat View Circle in the Twin Lakes condominium complex? This distance could have easily been covered at a leisurely pace in only fifteen to twenty minutes.

Closed circuit television (CCTV) surveillance video captures Trayvon purchasing Skittles and a can of Arizona Iced Tea at exactly 6:24:18 pm on the night immediately before the shooting. Trayvon's cell phone call to ex-girlfriend Rachael Jeantel, telling her that he was being followed (by Zimmerman), was made at 6:54 pm. This raises the question of what Martin was doing for that ten to fifteen-minute period. If the teen were new to the complex, why would he be walking down the dark side areas and away from the illuminated streets that led directly to his father's condo? And given the rain, why not take the most direct and well lighted route that would have been preferable to most people? Clearly, Martin did not do so.

This was some of the suspicious activity that attracted Zimmerman's attention. It certainly would have attracted the attention of any police officer on patrol. I am a former burglary suppression officer, and *I* would certainly have noticed it.

Who really pursued whom?

Another question that became controversial and of significant interest to the Zimmerman jury was the issue of just who pursued and engaged whom immediately before the shooting. State prosecutors and the media attempted to make George Zimmerman the aggressor, but this portrayal was not factually accurate.

There was and continues to be much non-forensic speculation that George Zimmerman "pursued" Trayvon Martin and, as I mentioned above, this was a major argument advanced by the state prosecutors during trial. It is certainly the mantra repeated and disseminated by Martin's supporters, including members of the Black Lives Matter movement. The problem here is that forensically and legally, this argument never held any water, and the jury did not buy it. Here are the empirical facts.

George Zimmerman admits to have followed Trayvon Martin both prior to and during his cell phone call to the Sanford PD Emergency 911 call center and operator. Zimmerman states that he followed Martin in an effort to determine what he was doing and his direction of travel through the complex. Police, prosecutors, and the jury had the transcript of Zimmerman's 911 call to Sanford PD, commencing at 7:09:34 pm and ending at 7:13:41 pm (lasting 04:07 minutes) and detailing his actions.

During the 911 call, Zimmerman reported that Martin suddenly turned around towards him and began to approach him with his hand inside his waistband. Zimmerman told the 911 operator this and then requested that an officer respond to his location. At this point, Zimmerman reports, Martin suddenly began running away, and he began to follow him. The 911 operator could tell by the ambient noise of running and Zimmerman's rapid, heavy breathing that he was following Martin on foot. At this point, the operator asked Zimmerman if he was following Martin, and Zimmerman confirmed that he was. The operator then told Zimmerman that the police did not need him to do so.

Zimmerman is then heard to respond, "OK" and at this moment, all ambient sounds of Zimmerman moving on the audio abruptly stops. The listener can hear on the audio recording that Zimmerman's voice and his breathing pattern have returned to normal and there is an absence of any sounds associated with rapid movement. The background sounds, including Zimmerman's breathing pattern and footsteps on the 911 audio tape, support Zimmerman's representation to police that he had in fact stopped following and was returning at a normal gait back to his truck.

We also know, from forensically analyzing the cell phone records of Trayvon Martin and his former girlfriend Rachael Jeantel, that Martin first called her at 6:54 pm and had an eighteen-minute conversation with her that ended at 7:12 pm. It was during this first call that he told Jeantel that a "creepy white cracker" had been following him. He next called Jeantel at 7:16 pm for 59 seconds, and his call abruptly and inexplicably dropped at 7:16:59 pm.

By comparing Zimmerman's 911 call audio, the voice transcripts, and the call times (which can be forensically established and thus referred to as "direct evidence") to Martin's and Jeantel's cell phone records and Jeantel's trial statements, we know that Zimmerman *did not pursue or accost* Trayvon Martin immediately prior to the confrontation and shooting. In fact, quite the opposite is true. It was actually Trayvon Martin who turned back towards George Zimmerman *a second time* and confronted and then violently assaulted Zimmerman.

Again, the forensic facts that can be proven are:

1. George Zimmerman was not following Trayvon Martin after the 911 operator advised him not to.
2. It was actually Martin who turned around twice and physically confronted and physically engaged Zimmerman.
3. If Trayvon Martin was ever concerned about Zimmerman following him, he certainly did not continue to vacate the area by fleeing from Zimmerman, as Zimmerman had initially reported to the 911 operator at 7:11:33 pm that night.
4. If Trayvon Martin was concerned for his safety because someone was following him, he never called the Sanford PD 911 emergency call center, as any concerned citizen would do.

The Florida state prosecutors did not have to explain Trayvon's actions because they never considered him to be anything other than the "victim" during their investigation and prosecution of Zimmerman. This was just one of a number of fatal flaws in the State's investigation and prosecution of Zimmerman. However, to compound matters and the challenges the prosecutors already faced, Judge Nelson clearly did not want to have "victim" Trayvon and his past history put on trial.

The jurist allowed the prosecutors to continue to advance their ridiculous and factually and forensically unsupported theory that George Zimmerman first "racially profiled" and then pursued and attacked Trayvon Martin. There is no doubt that this seriously flawed theory of so-called criminal intent created more than a little skepticism in the minds of the jurors who were slowly but surely beginning to connect the dots.

So who really confronted and assaulted whom?

Forensic evidence was available from the 911 audio and at least one "ear witness" who called the Sanford PD 911 emergency call center to report noises outside of his condominium. In one audio recording, screams can be heard leading to the sudden report of a single gunshot.

The first ear witness' 911 call commences at 7:16:11 pm. This is only eleven seconds after Trayvon Martin's final cell phone call to Rachael Jeantel was disconnected. That is interesting and important.

We now know from the direct, forensic evidence of George Zimmerman's medical reports, supported by color photographs of the injuries to his head and face; that it is far more likely than not that the younger, much stronger, faster, and physically fit six-foot, 158-pound former football player Martin suddenly and violently attacked the smaller, heavier and out of shape 5'-7", 194 pound Zimmerman. In use of force parlance, this is commonly referred to as "disparity of force."

Color photographs of Zimmerman taken at the scene and later at the Sanford PD station clearly showed George Zimmerman with two swollen black eyes and bleeding facial injuries that included a fractured and swollen nose, along with numerous bleeding lacerations to the back of his head with significant swelling present there.

It is important to note that the state prosecutors deliberately withheld several of these critical and potentially exculpatory photos from Zimmerman's defense team for a period of two months following the incident.

Trayvon Martin's autopsy report and injury diagram document abrasions to the knuckles of his left hand. Other than a single intermediate range gunshot wound (GSW) to the left side of his chest and the associated penetrative wounds commonly associated with a projectile creating a typical wound channel through the cardio-respiratory area, Martin's body is absent any other remarkable trauma. In other words, he had no other injuries. However, what *is* remarkable is that the abrasions noted to his left hand are consistent with his balled up fist being the mechanism of George Zimmerman's facial injuries.

Conversely, George Zimmerman's hands, knuckles, arms and body showed *no evidence* of any abrasions or marks that would be consistent with striking Trayvon Martin. Neither did Zimmerman's body display any evidence of defensive wounds inflicted by Martin. The knees of Zimmerman's pants showed no evidence of concrete abrasion consistent with Zimmerman being on top of Martin during the fight. However, Trayvon Martin's pants did show evidence of such concrete abrasions.

These facts provide conclusive forensic evidence that supports Zimmerman's statement to police that Martin was on top of him, in what is referred to in mixed martial arts parlance as a "front mount position," while violently attacking him.

Zimmerman told police that Martin had turned around, approached, accosted and then suddenly punched him in the face. According to Zimmerman, after punching him and knocking him to the cement sidewalk and on his back, Martin then mounted him from the front and began to rain down violent punches to his face. Zimmerman told police that in the process, Martin grabbed his head and began to repeatedly pound the back of his head into the cement pavement.

Independent witness John Good testifies.

Perhaps the most critical witness in the trial was neighbor John Good, who provided key testimony indicating that it was Zimmerman and not Trayvon who was on the ground and being pummeled mixed-martial-arts-style by an assailant (Martin). Good told the jury, "I could tell that the person on the bottom had a lighter skin color and was wearing what appeared to be white or red [clothing], while the person on top [of him] wore dark clothing."[5]

As the public and the jury already knew, on the night of the incident it was Zimmerman who was wearing a red windbreaker type of jacket. Trayvon Martin was the person dressed in dark clothing. Witness Good's testimony also supported the mechanisms of injury sustained by Zimmerman to his face and the back of his head. Poor crime scene processing and the inept handling and processing of evidence by Sanford PD officers, investigators and the Coroner's Office, unfortunately, destroyed blood transfer evidence between Martin and Zimmerman.

The prosecution's portrayal of a supposedly "scared" Trayvon Martin using what was forensically proven to be excessive and potentially deadly force upon George Zimmerman apparently did not resonate with the jury after they had listened to the testimony of witness Good.

The jurors had viewed photos of Zimmerman's injuries and had heard medical experts testifying on Zimmerman's injuries and the potential for him to be seriously injured or killed by Martin. They had also seen the clothing worn by both men at the time of the incident. Therefore, the prosecutors had to attempt to deflect witness Good and the defense medical experts by using their medical expert Dr. Valeria Rao, who argued that Zimmerman's injuries "were not life threatening."

Testimony of forensic pathologist Dr. Vincent DiMaio

The defense countered with eminent forensic pathologist Dr. Vincent DiMaio, a former Chief Medical Examiner in Texas, who is renowned as an expert in force-related injuries and ballistics and gunshot wounds. Dr. DiMaio was able to prove to the jury the obvious: that Martin

---

[5] Wit. John Good's trial testimony.
https://www.youtube.com/watch?v=i1fgmWEfSf4

repeatedly bashing Zimmerman's skull into the concrete pavement could cause a serious and potentially fatal injury.

Further, Dr. DiMaio testified that all of the evidence he had reviewed with respect to Zimmerman's injuries was consistent with the manner and mechanisms of injury described by both Zimmerman and witness John Good to police after the shooting. Dr. DiMaio assured the jurors that it was more than possible for a person to receive severe and life threatening traumatic injury to the head without the presence of significant visible injuries.

Even more damaging to the prosecution's case, Dr. DiMaio testified that that the bullet wound and trajectory of the single 9mm projectile fired by Zimmerman into Martin's upper torso was completely consistent with Zimmerman's account of how he had drawn his Kel-Tec 9mm semi-automatic pistol from a right side in-the-waistband holster when he fired the weapon at close range into the slight left side of Martin's chest while on his back and being violently beaten by the teen.

Dr. DiMaio testified that the location of Trayvon Martin's gunshot wound and the bullet's trajectory through his body indicated that Zimmerman had fired the weapon from a distance of between two and four inches; with the gun's muzzle in close proximity to Martin's clothing. [6]

Dr. DiMaio testified, quite simply, that "If you lean over someone, you notice that the clothing tends to fall away from the chest. If instead, you're lying on your back and someone shoots you, the clothing is going to be against your chest."[7]

---

[6]https://en.wikipedia.org/wiki/Shooting_of_Trayvon_Martin#County_medical_examiner.27s_autopsy_report

[7] Dr. Vincent DiMaio Zimmerman trial testimony

The pathologist's testimony to the jury was basic, simply stated and easy to understand and was an excellent presentation of medical evidence.

Dr. DiMaio's findings and opinions were also consistent with physical force injuries I have personally investigated. Medical, law enforcement, and martial arts professionals readily understand and agree that anyone whose head is being pummeled while his skull is positioned on a hard surface such as a cement sidewalk can easily sustain what is referred to as a "contra coup" injury. This type of injury can be potentially fatal even without the presence of significant visible injuries such as deep bleeding lacerations. Emergency room physicians and child abuse investigators are aware that infants are the frequent victims of serious injury and death from "shaken baby syndrome," where there is no outward evidence of traumatic injury.

Self-defense law supports Zimmerman's actions.

What was equally important in the Zimmerman trial is that Florida self-defense law states only that a person being assaulted must have a reasonable belief that his assailant's actions could cause serious bodily injury or death at the time he uses deadly force. [8]

State Prosecutors: Zimmerman displayed "malice aforethought." Really? When?

The state prosecutors were never able to present any credible evidence that George Zimmerman demonstrated any "malice aforethought" that would constitute an element of the crime of 2nd-degree murder. What was never discussed by either side at trial is what I will discuss with you now. Zimmerman's Kel-Tec 9mm semi-automatic pistol held a magazine containing seven more rounds.

---

[8] FL Statute Title XLVI, Ch. 776, §§776.012(1); 776.013

If Zimmerman was clearly and maliciously intent upon confronting, engaging, and killing Martin, why didn't he fire *multiple* rounds into Trayvon's body when he clearly had the ability to do so? Homicide investigators classically see evidence of what is referred to as "overkill" in real murders where anger, rage, and malice are present. Instead, in this case, it appears that Zimmerman displayed a reluctant desperation to simply stop Martin's violent assault upon him.

One could certainly and appropriately argue that Zimmerman fired one shot into Martin in the heat of combat, assessed Martin's reaction to being shot, and then stopped firing because he had successfully stopped Martin's threat.

Clearly, there was no evidence of any "excessive use of deadly force" by Zimmerman. In the incidents involving police officers I have investigated involving similar circumstances, the officers justifiably fired multiple rounds into suspects to stop their potentially deadly force threat. Why was the Zimmerman shooting investigated any differently than any officer-involved shooting?

Much posturing about nothing: No "stand your ground" defense was presented by Zimmerman's defense team.

There has been much national discussion and posturing by politicians, the Florida State Prosecutors, anti-gun advocates, and media sympathetic to Trayvon Martin regarding the "stand your ground" provision in Florida's Justifiable Use of Force/Deadly Force statute. In reality, the Zimmerman case was never about the "duty to retreat" component of that law. Judge Nelson was required to read Florida's "Justifiable Use of Force" statute, including the "no requirement to retreat" element to the jury during jury instructions.

However, the "stand your ground" provision was *never* part of Zimmerman's defense. Please do not allow yourself to be beguiled by this specious and totally irrelevant argument. It's nothing but smoke and mirrors.

The realities of the State of Florida vs. George Zimmerman case were:

1. George Zimmerman was a private citizen on private property, in a place he had a legal right to be when Trayvon Martin confronted and violently assaulted him.
2. Zimmerman had legal standing and entrusted authority, as the Twin Lakes HOA's appointed Neighborhood Watch Captain, to observe, identify, and report on suspicious persons and criminal behavior.
3. Zimmerman had a legal right to observe, follow, and report upon Martin's suspicious behavior. Just like any private security guard, he was also well within his legal rights and the law to consensually encounter and converse with anyone within the condominium complex to identify him and determine his purpose for being on private property. Zimmerman *violated no laws,* and the jury agreed.

The evidence shows that Trayvon Martin's encounter with and assault upon George Zimmerman was apparently so sudden and devastating that Zimmerman never had an opportunity to retreat before being punched in the face, knocked backside down on a cement sidewalk, mounted mixed-martial-arts style, and repeatedly and violently pummeled by Martin. There is no doubt that these factors weighed heavily in the jury's ultimate decision to acquit George Zimmerman.

The Florida State Prosecutors, no doubt with the assistance of the incredible resources of the U.S. Department of Justice, spent sixteen months wrangling, posturing, and, I believe, unethically concealing exculpatory evidence. This was followed by more public posturing, legal bickering and weeks of trial testimony with the aid of a sympathetic judge who ruled in the prosecution's favor at nearly every step of the way.

Ultimately, the state prosecutors were unable to present any type of viable strategy or credible arguments to overcome the significant evidence and the jury's more than reasonable doubt that George Zimmerman was guilty of *any* crimes. As we all watched on television, it appeared as if the majority of the prosecution's best witnesses gave testimony in one way or another actually supporting the defense team's arguments.

Zimmerman defense attorney Mark O'Mara calmly, deliberately, and methodically eviscerated the prosecution's case against his client. After O'Mara's summation, including his use of the prosecution's own stage props to prove their self-defense argument, the prosecution's case against George Zimmerman appeared to collapse.

Upon the conclusion of the trial, the jury unanimously found Zimmerman innocent of all charges. Rather than resigning with the knowledge that they presented the only type of case that they were capable of, given the circumstances, and encouraging the public and media to move forward, the prosecutors remained adamant that Zimmerman murdered Martin in cold blood.

Case and Trial Summary

Any opinions or speculation as to what George Zimmerman "would-a, could-a, or should-a" done that night are completely irrelevant to the above fact pattern, the criminal charges that were filed against him, and the ultimate criminal elements and legal standards of proof in his trial. This was a *criminal* and not a *civil* trial, so please don't attempt to apply an incorrect standard of proof in your analysis of the "totality of circumstances" of this case.

My opinion is that the Zimmerman investigation became a "political shooting" to which a double standard was applied and a black teen assailant became the "victim" instead of the suspect. From the very beginning, a shoddy investigation was initiated by officers and investigators and led by state prosecutors, who made a faulty determination of criminal culpability and then sought to wrap a poorly framed investigation around their incorrect assessment while ignoring and then deliberately concealing critical facts and forensic evidence that were exculpatory to George Zimmerman.

Both the investigators and their prosecutor counterparts just kept trying to hammer a square peg into a round hole all the way to the last day of trial. Simply speaking, had it not been for a unique defense team of professional trial attorneys and forensic experts who were able to peel back the layers of the onion of deceit and misdirection - and an intelligent jury - the Zimmerman trial would have more than likely resulted in a complete miscarriage of justice and denial of due process for the beleaguered defendant.

One lesson to be learned from this trial debacle and a near miscarriage of justice is that conceit and arrogance are no substitute for honesty, truth, and direct forensic evidence. Politically correct rhetoric and political posturing have no place in a courtroom of law - or in a nation governed by the rule of law. Ultimately, when exculpatory facts and evidence are present, and the right people with heroic courage, stamina and tenacity are in place to stringently fight against false narratives, justice prevails.

As law enforcement, forensic, and legal professionals, we are often faced with difficult cases and fact patterns that lack criminal elements, or we lack the legal foundation to help injured parties who come to us for "justice" to move forward, towards resolution and closure. The unfortunate reality for the parents of Trayvon Martin and members of the Black Lives Matter movement is that if you do not accept objective facts, forensic evidence, and jury verdicts, you will always believe that the system was "unjust" to you, and no amount of evidence or sympathy will assuage you.

I admit that I have been involved in a number of emotionally draining cases where I questioned the decision of a judge or a jury. I have left more than one courtroom shaking my head and trying to figure out the mindset of a trier of fact.

In this case, I believe that the circumstances and evidence were overwhelmingly exculpatory to George Zimmerman. The problem was that the media, Martin's family, and the politics of race drove the prosecution of this case. While Zimmerman may have made a poor decision to follow Trayvon Martin, it was ultimately Martin who was criminally culpable of engaging and violently assaulting the weaker Zimmerman. Unfortunately, Martin forfeited his life for making that mistake.

Future "prosecutions" of George Zimmerman? Fact vs. fantasy

As I initially opined in a lengthy 2013 forensic article following the jury's acquittal of George Zimmerman ("The Zimmerman Verdict – A Victory of the Rule of Law over Politics"), the chance that the U.S. Department of Justice would criminally prosecute George Zimmerman in the death of Trayvon Martin was nil.

On February 24, 2015, the DOJ issued a press release advising that its "independent investigation found 'insufficient evidence' to charge George Zimmerman with any federal civil rights violations in the shooting death of Florida teen Trayvon Martin." [9] End of story.

---

[9] http://www.usatoday.com/story/news/2015/02/24/no-federals-charges-against-george-zimmerman/23942297/

Chapter 3

"Hands up! Don't shoot!"
Michael Brown vs. Officer Darren Wilson
The forensic facts behind the officer-involved shooting (OIS) in Ferguson, MO

Preface

Much of the information in this chapter has been gleaned from the March 4, 2015 report of the United States Department of Justice (USDOJ) following its extensive and exhaustive investigation of the officer-involved fatal shooting of suspect Michael Brown by Ferguson, MO Patrol Officer Darren Wilson on August 9, 2014. A number of quotes that appear in this chapter have been taken directly from this report and are appropriately referenced. For the sake of investigative confidentiality, the report identifies witnesses only by number, rather than their names. If you want to see the 86-page report for yourself, it's easily available on the Internet. [10]

The Circumstances

On a warm and sunny morning, shortly before noon in Ferguson, Missouri, a northern suburb of St. Louis, 18-year-old Michael Brown and his companion Dorian Johnson entered the Ferguson Market & Liquor, a small family-owned convenience store known by locals as "The Ferguson Market."

_____

[10] http://www.justice.gov/sites/default/files/opa/press-releases/attachments/2015/03/04/doj_report_on_shooting_of_michael_brown_1.pdf

The Indian victim store clerk would later report to investigators - and the store's video surveillance system would forensically confirm - that while in the store Michael Brown asked the clerk for a package of cigarillos. When the clerk produced the cigarillos and placed them on the counter, Brown suddenly snatched them up and handed them to Johnson. Brown then reached over the counter and grabbed several more packages of cigarillos. When the clerk asked for payment, Brown refused. Johnson then placed the cigarillos Brown had handed him on the counter, and Brown picked those up as well and began to exit the store.

When the 5'6" clerk attempted to hold the front door closed to keep the 6'4", 292-pound Brown from exiting the store with the merchandise, Brown responded by menacingly approaching the clerk and threatening, "What are you going to do about it?" Brown then forcefully shoved the clerk aside and walked boldly out of the store.

Brown's behavior inside the store was no mere "petty theft," as has been reported in the media and by Brown apologists. As the law clearly states, and as police officers are trained, any theft accomplished by force or fear is classified as a "robbery." All robberies are felonies. In this case, Michael Brown accomplished his theft of the cigarillos by both physical force and fear. He was unarmed at the time, so this crime would be classified as a "strong-armed robbery" - but a felony nonetheless.

The store clerk's daughter, who had witnessed the incident, called 911 to report the theft and provide a physical and clothing description of Brown and Johnson.

Officer Wilson's encounter with Michael Brown

At the same time of the strong-armed robbery at the Ferguson Market, 28-year-old Ferguson Police Officer Darren Wilson was on patrol in the neighborhood, driving a fully-marked and equipped, department-issued Chevy Tahoe SUV. At the time, Officer Wilson was dressed in full police uniform and wearing a duty belt equipped with his Sig Sauer S&W .40 caliber semi-automatic pistol, an ASP expandable baton, a canister of OC pepper spray, and handcuffs.

Officer Wilson had heard a recent police broadcast of a "Stealing in Progress" at the Ferguson Market, along with a description of the two subjects involved. As Officer Wilson drove westbound on Canfield Drive, he observed Brown and Johnson walking eastbound down the middle of the street on the median line in traffic. The officer observed that several vehicles were forced to drive around the pair to avoid them. A pedestrian walking dangerously in the middle of the roadway is a violation of the Missouri vehicle code and is classified as a citable infraction.

Officer Wilson drove up to Brown and Johnson and instructed them to get out of the roadway and onto the safety of the sidewalk. Witness Johnson told investigators that when Wilson directed them to get onto the sidewalk, Johnson replied that they were almost at their destination.

Officer Wilson then inquired, "What's wrong with the sidewalk?" Wilson told investigators that when he had directed the two men out of the roadway, Brown angrily responded, "Fuck what you have to say!" At the same time, he observed that Brown was holding a package of cigarillos in his hand and noted that both men matched the descriptions of the suspects involved in the recent theft at the nearby Ferguson Market.

Officer Wilson made a determination to detain Brown and Johnson to investigate whether or not they had been involved in the theft. At that moment, he was not aware how Brown had committed the theft. For purposes of officer safety, Wilson requested the assistance of other officers by radioing to police dispatch, "Put me on Canfield with two and send me another car."

Officer Wilson then positioned his SUV at an angle blocking both lanes of traffic and blocking Brown and Johnson's path. This was the point of detention. Police officers are trained that in order to be able to stop, detain and possibly search people, they must have at least "reasonable suspicion," generally defined by various court rulings, as specific, articulable circumstances and facts which would cause a trained officer to reasonably believe that criminal activity has either taken place, is taking place, or will take place, and there is a connection between that activity and the person(s) to be stopped.

The three kinds of police encounters

In law enforcement, police have three distinct kinds of encounters with the public: (1) a consensual encounter, (2) a detention, and (3) an arrest.

First, the "consensual encounter." Police are trained that a police officer can approach any citizen in a public area at any time of the day or night without consent, reasonable suspicion, or probable cause. During this encounter, a police officer may ask the citizen questions, make requests, and perhaps even give the citizen simple instructions such as asking him to step out of a roadway or to remove his hands from his pockets for safety.

Officers are trained that the key element in a consensual encounter, absent the elements needed to detain or arrest, is that both officer and citizen must *consent* to having this encounter. If the citizen decides that he does not want to converse with an officer and there is no reasonable suspicion or probable cause for the officer to detain or arrest him, the citizen is free to simply decline the encounter and go about his business without fear of any lawful enforcement action. However, it is also important to point out that it is ultimately the officer and not the citizen who controls any citizen contact, and the street is not the place to argue or resist any encounter that might transition into a detention. That is why we have courts of law.

Officers are trained that any time they encounter a citizen and issue specific instructions, directions, orders, or commands or act in any way that would lead the citizen to reasonably conclude that he is no longer free to go about his business and is required to comply with the officer's directions and/or commands, this constitutes a "detention."

Detentions, like arrests, are protected by the Constitution's 4th Amendment guidelines, which protect citizens against "unreasonable searches and seizures." As just discussed, the *minimum* legal and Constitutional standard for police to detain a citizen is *reasonable* suspicion.

It is important to know that not all detentions are "stop and frisks," in which an officer might also conduct a cursory search of a citizen for weapons.

Under circumstances that might warrant such a search, also referred to as a "Terry Stop," from the U.S. Supreme Court case of *Terry v. Ohio (1968),* officers are trained that they cannot search every citizen they detain just because they want to. In order to search a citizen for the presence of a weapon, officers must have an *objectively reasonable* belief that the person presents a threat to their safety and/or may be in possession of a concealed weapon that could be used to harm them. [11]

Officers are trained that cursory or "Terry Searches" are limited in scope to external, non-intrusive or "outer body" searches of a citizen's person for weapons only. Officers are taught that cursory searches are not to be used as what the courts refer to as a "fishing expedition" for non-weapon contraband. [12]

The last encounter that an officer may have with a citizen is a physical arrest. Arrests are accomplished by either the advisement that the citizen is under arrest and/or the physical touching of that person, coupled with the citizen's submission to custody. Officers are trained that "probable cause" is the minimum Constitutional standard required for any arrest. "Probable cause" is generally defined as specific,

---

[12] Case cite: Terry v. Ohio, 392, U.S. 1 (1968)

articulable circumstances and facts that lead a trained officer to reasonably conclude that a person has committed a crime.

Reasonable suspicion and probable cause

While the definitions of "reasonable suspicion" and "probable cause" sound similar, they are actually not. Both are objective and forensic, rather than subjective standards of proof. It is very important for police officers to differentiate between the two. When officers make mistakes in the field, this is usually the first one they make.

So what is the difference between these two standards of proof? A subjective standard is merely one's speculative opinion or belief, whereas an objective standard requires specific, articulable circumstances, statements, facts and/or forensic evidence that can be repeatedly tested and compared.

The U. S. Supreme Court has set down Constitutional, 4th Amendment guidelines, according to which police officers cannot base their detentions or arrests of citizens upon a *subjective* standard of proof – that is, they cannot use mere suspicions, hunches, or even "educated guesses" as the *sole* basis for detaining or arresting citizens.

It is always important for good field officers to be vigilant and hyper-aware of suspicious activity. In fact, the courts allow trained and certified police officers more latitude than non-trained civilian private citizens in applying their suspicions to their "collective knowledge" in making a determination as to whether or not reasonable suspicion or probable cause exists to detain or arrest someone.

"Collective knowledge" is generally defined as an officer's education, training and experience, including his moment-by-moment observations and experience of what is happening.

However, in the end, the courts *require* that officers always have at least the minimum legal standard needed to affect a detention or arrest. They also mandate that police officers always act with "objective reasonableness" when taking any enforcement action(s) that may negatively affect a citizen's constitutionally protected rights against unreasonable searches and seizures.

It is also critically important for citizens to understand and comply with state statutes and Constitutional case laws whenever they have an encounter with police. These laws are specifically designed to inform citizens that it is a criminal offense to delay, obstruct, or resist any peace officer in the lawful performance of his duty. In fact, even if a detention or arrest is unlawful on its face, *citizens have absolutely no lawful right to resist* that detention or arrest.

It is also important that citizens understand that when making determinations as to a citizen's criminal culpability following an arrest for resisting arrest, the courts do not take into account a citizen's defense that he resisted the officer(s) merely because the defendant *thought* that the officer had no right to detain or arrest. Judges understand that a court of law and not the street is the appropriate venue for arguing the legality of an officer's stop, traffic citation, investigative detention, or arrest.

Why were Brown and Johnson detained in the first place?

A consistent theme in literally *all* of the incidents of police uses of force, officer-involved shootings and in-custody deaths criticized by members of the Black Lives Matter movement is that the initial police detention of a black citizen is always capricious, racially profiled, and/or without cause and unlawful.

Leaders of the BLM movement and supporter activists made these same accusations against Officer Darren Wilson in their criticism of his initial stop and attempt to detain Michael Brown and Dorian Johnson.

In the Brown case, Officer Wilson had more than sufficient circumstances, facts, and evidence to stop and detain both Brown and Johnson. First, his on-view violation of the infraction of two pedestrians walking in the middle of the roadway obstructing traffic - a citable offense. Next, the officer had sufficient "collective knowledge" that both men who matched their physical descriptions were possibly involved in the theft at the Ferguson Market just moments before.

Officer Wilson had heard a police radio broadcast of the recent theft of cigarillos from the Ferguson Market, with a description of two black men that matched the physical descriptions of Brown and Johnson. He was aware that both men were walking from the direction of the market and specifically observed that Brown was in possession of a package of cigarillos. This is referred to as the "temporal relationship" between a crime location, a time interval, and possible involved suspects.

State criminal and federal civil rights case laws are clear that Officer Wilson was well within his legal scope and authority to stop, detain and question Brown and Johnson to determine whether or not they were involved in the Ferguson Market theft. This was one of the first key determinations that the U.S. Department of Justice attorneys made in favor of Officer Darren Wilson when they reviewed the circumstances of his encounter with Michael Brown.

Officer Wilson apparently pulled his SUV in too close to Michael Brown, which did not allow the officer enough distance to exit his vehicle safely. When the officer attempted to open his driver's side door, it either came into contact with Brown's body, or Brown slammed it back shut so Officer Wilson could not exit his vehicle.

Officer Wilson told investigators that it was Brown who deliberately slammed the door on him. The officer states that he told Brown to "Get back!" and tried again to open the door, but Brown placed his hands on the door frame so that Wilson could not open it.

Officer Wilson violently assaulted in his patrol car

Officer Wilson and nearby witnesses told investigators that they then observed Michael Brown hand the cigarillos he was holding to Johnson and then suddenly reach into the open driver's side window of Officer Wilson's SUV and grab and pummel the officer.

Officer Wilson stated that Brown was "swinging wildly" at him and punched him in the jaw twice, while grabbing onto his uniform shirt, neck, hands and arms. The officer's and witnesses' statements are forensically corroborated by photographs of the bruising to Wilson's jaw, scratches on his neck, the presence of Brown's DNA on Officer Wilson's uniform shirt, collar, and pants, and the officer's DNA found on the palm of Michael Brown's hand.

Officer Wilson told investigators that he responded to Brown's violent assault by unholstering his sidearm and pointing it at Brown because the manner of Brown's assault and Wilson's position while seated and trapped inside his patrol SUV precluded him from accessing his less than lethal defensive weaponry (OC pepper spray, flash light and ASP baton).

A desperate fight over control of Officer Wilson's pistol

The investigation determined that during the assault, Brown grabbed onto Wilson's semi-automatic pistol and began struggling with the officer in an attempt to disarm him. Wilson yelled that he would shoot Brown if Brown did not release the gun. Brown responded, "You're too much of a pussy to shoot!" and then placed his hand over Wilson's right hand that was holding the pistol to gain better control of the weapon.

During the struggle, Brown managed to redirect the muzzle of the pistol down towards Wilson's left hip. Brown's size and superior physical position left the officer completely vulnerable to being shot. At this dire point, he managed to brace his left elbow against the door to create sufficient leverage over Brown to be able to re-direct the muzzle of his pistol back towards the driver's side door, on which Brown was leaning.

Officer Wilson, in defense of his life, pulled the trigger twice. But the gun would not fire because Brown had his hand over the slide of the weapon - which no doubt prevented the gun from functioning properly. When Wilson yanked on the pistol and depressed the trigger a third time, the gun finally fired.

When his weapon discharged, Wilson immediately heard the glass from the retracted door window shatter and saw blood on his hand. Brown appeared to be momentarily startled and backed up and put his right hand down to his right hip. Wilson states that he knew that he had fired through his driver's side door, so he assumed that his first round had struck Brown.

Officer Wilson told investigators that after only a brief moment, Brown became enraged and "looked like a demon." Brown immediately re-engaged by leaning back into the driver's side door with his head and arms back inside the driver's compartment and then assaulted him a second time. Wilson describes a chaotic and desperate situation, as he attempted to shield his face with his left hand to fend off Brown's powerful blows, while attempting to fire his gun. But his gun jammed.

He then managed to lift up his gun again towards his assailant, and then used both hands to manually clear his pistol and successfully fire a second shot at Brown. Wilson did not see if his round had struck Brown and does not think it did; he then saw Brown run away.

"Shots fired!"

Officer Wilson and witnesses state that when Brown fled, the officer radioed "Shots fired!" and again requested immediate assistance. Wilson then pursued Brown on foot. When investigators asked Wilson why he had given chase instead of disengaging, the officer told them that given the fact that Brown had just attacked and attempted to kill a police officer, he felt that Brown posed a serious threat to anyone with whom he would have come into contact.

Brown turns and runs towards Officer Wilson.

The statements of Officer Wilson, supported by credible witnesses and forensic evidence, indicates that the officer chased after Brown while holding his pistol in the "low ready" position and yelling after Brown to "Stop and get on the ground!" Brown ignored the repeated orders and from a distance of thirty feet suddenly turned around to face Wilson.

Officer Wilson described Brown's expression at this moment as "psychotic," "hostile," and "crazy," as if Brown were "looking through" him. Wilson also told investigators that Brown was "making a grunting noise" while displaying "the most intense and aggressive face that [he] had ever seen a person make." Just as suddenly as Brown had turned to face Officer Wilson, he began running directly towards him. In response, Wilson began to disengage backwards with his weapon at the ready, while again repeatedly yelling at Brown to stop and get on the ground.

The issue of "disparity of force"

Officer Wilson's statements, supported by credible witnesses and forensic evidence, show that rather than complying, Brown continued running towards him. Wilson was in fear of his life and had run out of options. He was already keenly aware that Brown had not only just violently assaulted him but had also attempted to disarm and shoot him. Given Michael Brown's large stature and bizarre, aggressive behavior, Officer Wilson also had good reason to believe that Brown was also under the influence of drugs. These are all elements that point to Michael Brown's "disparity of force" over Officer Wilson.

In their use-of-force classes, police officers are trained that the issue of a resistant subject's "disparity of force" can form part of the calculus of an officer's defensive force response to stop an imminent threat of great bodily harm. Officer Wilson told investigators that he realized that had Brown been able to reach him, "[he] would have been done."

Brown charges; Officer Wilson responds with deadly force.

As Wilson was backing up and yelling at Brown to stop, he saw Brown reach into his waistband, which was concealed by his shirt. In response to Brown's charge and furtive movement, he fired because he believed that Brown was reaching for a weapon.

The officer told investigators that Brown paused momentarily, which provided an opportunity to stop firing, briefly assess Brown's reaction and again yell at Brown to get on the ground. But instead of complying, Brown charged again, with his hand back inside of his waistband.

In response to the perceived weapon threat, Wilson fired at Brown again. When this did not stop the assailant, Wilson backed up and fired a third and final volley of shots at Brown when the subject was only about eight to ten feet away. Wilson told investigators that he observed his very last round penetrate the top of Brown's head, as Brown was charging in a crouched and running position "as if [Brown] was going to tackle [him]," and Brown immediately went down.

Officer Wilson recalls firing a volley of five shots, then two shots, and a final volley that ultimately mortally wounded Brown.

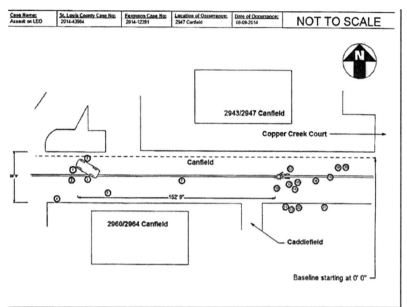

Case Name: Assault on LEO	St. Louis County Case No: 2014-43984	Ferguson Case No: 2014-12391	Location of Occurrence: 2947 Canfield	Date of Occurrence: 08-09-2014

2943/2947 Canfield

Copper Creek Court

Canfield

152' 9"

2960/2964 Canfield

Caddiefield

Baseline starting at 0' 0"

St. Louis County Sheriff's Office Crime Scene Diagram of Brown OIS

Investigation findings and case forensics

A number of "witnesses" came forward to make statements to the news media and investigators that discounted Officer Wilson's account of this incident. However, the FBI and other municipal law enforcement investigators never found any credible evidence to disprove Wilson's account of what happened inside the police SUV or outside the vehicle during his encounter with Michael Brown.

As briefly discussed, although some witnesses claimed that Brown's hands were never inside Officer Wilson's patrol SUV, both forensic evidence of Brown's DNA found inside the SUV and on Officer Wilson's shirt collar, as well as the bullet trajectory and close-range gunshot wound to Brown's hand, clearly establish that Brown's upper torso, arms and hands were in fact inside the patrol SUV. The accounts of credible witnesses also support the forensic evidence and Officer Wilson's account.

The forensic evidence shows that after being initially shot in the hand by Officer Wilson at the SUV, Michael Brown ran at least 180 feet from the police unit. DNA evidence confirms that Brown left a blood trail of this distance as he fled from the officer. Brown then turned around and ran back towards Officer Wilson before being shot and falling to his death on the roadway, approximately 21.6 feet west of the blood in the roadway. Some witness accounts that Brown never moved back towards Officer Wilson were not reconciled or supported by the contradicting DNA evidence. Therefore, those witness statements were not relied upon by the prosecution.

As discussed at length in the FBI's report of the shooting incident, several credible witnesses stated that Michael Brown appeared to pose a physical threat to Officer Wilson as he ran towards the officer. Officer Wilson states that he feared that Brown would again assault him because of Brown's behavior at the SUV patrol unit and because Brown was moving rapidly towards him while ignoring numerous commends to "Stop! Get on the ground!"

Officer Wilson also observed Brown to be continually reaching under his shirt and into his waistband with his left hand as he rapidly moved towards him. Officers are taught in their officer safety classes that *eighty-five percent of all weapons found concealed on suspects are recovered from the waistband*. Another fact: suspects access concealed weapons to wound or kill officers in thirty-six percent of all officer-down incidents. While no weapon was ever found on Michael Brown, still, on the basis of Officer Wilson's training and what he was experiencing at the time, it was not unreasonable for him, before firing on Brown, to have heightened suspicions that Brown might also be attempting to access a weapon.

Time and distance compression was a major factor in the case analysis.

For context to the reader, it is important to understand the effects that time and distance have on any confrontation between resistive or violent subjects and the police officer(s) who are trying to isolate, contain, capture and control them. The compression of both time and distance can easily and quickly change the paradigm of an encounter. That's what happened in this case.

The chronology of this event has been documented and shows that Michael Brown committed his strong-arm robbery at the Ferguson Market at 11:53 hours (store surveillance video time stamp). Officer Wilson contacted Brown and Johnson seven minutes later at approximately 12:00 pm. Officer Wilson radioed "Shots fired!" only two minutes later, at 12:02 pm (police radio time stamp).

In the roughly two minutes of Officer Wilson's contact with Brown, Brown blocked the officer's exit from his patrol SUV, reached inside the vehicle, violently assaulted the officer, and grabbed onto and attempted to shoot the officer with his own gun. Officer Wilson managed to retain possession of his handgun, turned it back towards Brown, and fired, striking Brown in the right hand. Brown then fled from the patrol SUV with Wilson in brief foot pursuit, while yelling repeatedly at Brown to "Stop! Get on the ground!" Brown abruptly turned around to face the officer and then charged Wilson, who attempted to disengage from Brown to create more distance.

The statements of the officer, supported by credible witnesses and forensic evidence, conclusively shows that it was Brown who compressed time and distance on Officer Wilson. The first occasion was when Brown blocked the officer from getting out of his SUV and then assaulted him inside the vehicle. The second occasion was when Brown fled after being shot in the right hand and then suddenly turned towards the officer and charged him while Officer Wilson was backing away while ordering the very large and menacing Brown to stop and get on the ground.

It was ultimately Officer Wilson's recent and nearly deadly experience with Brown and Brown's charge that produced the reasonable fear in Wilson that Brown would seriously injure and/or disarm him and kill him that caused the officer to shoot Brown. A major component of Officer Wilson's fear was Brown's compression of the reactionary gap, with no time for Wilson to respond with anything less than lethal force to stop Brown's imminent threat.

Ballistics findings

Ballistics analysis confirmed that Officer Wilson discharged a total of twelve rounds at Michael Brown during the confrontation. Wilson fired two rounds at Brown at the patrol SUV and ten rounds during Brown's charge towards him on the roadway.

Witness accounts, supported by the forensic evidence of recorded cell phone audio, conclusively prove that Officer Wilson fired at Brown in three separate volleys, pausing between each volley. A review of Brown's autopsy shows that Brown sustained between six to eight bullet impacts, including one gunshot that passed through his right hand.

One fatal bullet strike to the apex of Brown's head resulted in instantaneous death, which caused Brown to immediately fall to the pavement within feet of the officer. Brown's autopsy report and the pathologist's diagram of bullet strikes to and trajectories of projectiles through Brown's body show *no evidence of any bullet strikes to Brown's back*.

As documented by crime scene photographs, Michael Brown fell to the ground with his left, uninjured hand balled up by his waistband and his right injured hand palm upwards by his side.

Autopsy diagram of bullet strikes to Michael Brown's torso

Questions and answers about the Michael Brown shooting incident

From the very day of the incident, numerous false statements, incorrect reports and false narratives have been generated. These incorrect, misstated, and or deliberately disingenuous false statements and reports have since been repeated in the news media, or by racial activists, plaintiff surrogates, and ultimately by the leaders, members and supporters of the Black Lives Matter movement, to promote their false narrative of the "extrajudicial killings" of young black men by police.

Here are the objective, non-speculative, forensic answers to many of the questions and statements that have been raised by the media and the BLM movement.

Officer Wilson wasn't aware that Michael Brown was involved in the theft at Ferguson Market when he stopped Brown and Johnson.

False. Forensic evidence of Ferguson PD police dispatch radio transmissions to patrol officers of a theft at the Ferguson Market, along with a description of the black male suspects, clearly supports Officer Wilson's account that he had heard the radio transmission regarding the theft and suspect descriptions at the time he stopped Brown and Johnson on Canfield Drive.

The physical and clothing descriptions in the police broadcast of two black males who turned out to be Michael Brown and his companion/ witness Dorian Johnson were consistent with the evidence found at the crime scene and the clothes worn by Brown and Johnson.

Officer Wilson reached outside of his patrol SUV, grabbed onto and choked Michael Brown during their initial encounter.

False. Brown's companion Dorian Johnson told investigators and the media that when Officer Wilson first encountered him and Brown, the officer reached outside the window of his patrol SUV and grabbed Brown by the neck and then commenced to choke him.

Three separate pathologists in three separate autopsies, including one by pathologist Dr. Michael Baden, who was retained by the Brown family, found no scratches, contusions, or any marks of trauma on or about Michael Brown's neck consistent with Officer Wilson grabbing and/or choking Brown.

DNA analysis of Michael Brown's clothes, right hand, and fingernails excluded Officer Wilson as a possible contributor.

Finally, investigators and prosecutors interviewing Johnson, other witnesses, and the forensic medical evidence determined Johnson's statements not to be credible or supported by the medical and DNA evidence.

Michael Brown never touched Officer Wilson or reached inside the patrol SUV during this incident.

False. As discussed, the statements of credible witnesses, supported by DNA evidence, conclusively prove that Brown repeatedly reached inside of Officer Wilson's patrol SUV and violently assaulted him. Witness Dorian Johnson, who was with Brown during the strong-arm robbery at the Ferguson Market, told police that Brown had never reached inside of the SUV and assaulted Officer Wilson. However, Johnson's statements were deemed not credible by prosecutors, in light of the forensic evidence, including injuries to the officer.

Michael Brown never struggled with Officer Wilson over control of the officer's pistol.

False. Pathologists in all three of Brown's autopsies, documented by photographs, diagrams and written reports, all note the presence of a graze or tangential wound to the base of Brown's right thumb, along with gunpowder soot. Soot appears in the vicinity of a gunshot wound when the muzzle of a weapon is within close ranges of one to three feet from point of impact.

Pathologists also found a thermal change in skin color or burning in the immediate vicinity of the gunshot wound to Brown's right hand. This is consistent with the extreme heat upon skin generated by the discharge of a firearm at very close ranges. Additionally, a piece of Brown's skin was recovered from the exterior of the driver's side door of Officer Wilson's patrol SUV that was consistent with the skin from the gunshot wound to Brown's right thumb.

The pathologists examining the gunshot wound to Brown's right hand determined that the presence of soot concentrated on only one side of the GSW, in combination with the tangential nature of the wound, and the bullet's trajectory through the thumb of the right hand, were consistent with the biomechanics of Michael Brown's right hand being on the slide and barrel, but not over the muzzle of Officer Wilson's pistol at the moment the officer discharged his weapon for the first time. This is significant forensic medical evidence that further corroborates Wilson's account that Brown struggled with him to gain control of his handgun in the patrol SUV.

Several witnesses told investigators that Brown was at or reaching inside of the driver's side of Officer Wilson's vehicle at the time that they heard the first gunshot. A spent bullet was also recovered from within the driver's side door of the SUV; this supported Wilson's statement regarding the dynamics of his struggle with Brown over control of his handgun.

Michael Brown's DNA was recovered at four significant locations in and about Officer Wilson's patrol SUV: on Wilson's gun; on the SUV driver's side door; inside the driver's side cockpit of the SUV; and on Wilson's uniform shirt. Additionally, a DNA mixture from which Officer Wilson's DNA could not be excluded was found on the palm of Brown's left hand. A DNA mixture found on the interior driver's side door handle revealed a major mixture profile that is *6.9 million* times more likely to be from Wilson and Brown than from Wilson and anyone else.

The FBI's report documents that analysis of the DNA found on Officer Wilson's pistol revealed a major mixture profile that is *2.1 octillion* times more likely a mixture of DNA from Wilson and Brown than from Wilson and anyone else. This is conclusive evidence that Brown's DNA was on Officer Wilson's gun.

Michael Brown was running away from Officer Wilson when he was shot. He never turned to face the officer and never charged towards Officer Wilson when he was shot.

False. Witness statements and crime scene evidence that included the positions of items of Michael Brown's clothing, a blood trail, DNA, the presence of spent bullet casings and the position of Brown's body only feet from where he was finally and fatally shot by Wilson are all consistent with and corroborate Officer Wilson's statements to investigators that Brown initially fled from the patrol SUV after being shot, then turned around, faced, and then charged Wilson at the moments he was repeatedly shot by the officer.

Witness statements alleging that Brown was shot by Wilson while Brown was running away and/or that Brown never approached Wilson in an aggressive manner were deemed not to be credible by investigators, nor were they supported by credible witness statements and the forensic evidence.

Although the exact order of the rounds fired at Michael Brown by Officer Wilson and bullet strikes to Brown's body cannot be exactly determined (with the exception of the first and last strikes), all of the gunshot wounds to Brown's body were to the front and right side. The absence of soot or stippling (burnt powder residue) in the vicinity of the bullet strikes indicates that with the exception of the wound to Brown's right hand, all rounds were fired from a distance beyond three feet. This forensic medical evidence is consistent with Michael Brown both facing and running towards Officer Wilson at the time that Wilson fired at Brown.

The shot to the apex of the top of Brown's head was the final and fatal shot. This bullet entered Brown's skull, at the base of the brain, and came to rest in the soft tissues on the right side of his face. This bullet strike to his central nervous system would have immediately killed Brown, given his position when struck. The trajectory or angle of this bullet as it passed through Brown's head was consistent with the biomechanics of Brown's body being bent at the waist and/or falling forward at the time he was shot.

DNA analysis of the blood trail found and documented on the pavement on Canfield Drive at the crime scene determined that two bloodstains observed and tested approximately seventeen and twenty-two feet east of where Michael Brown was fatally shot and fell were conclusively tied to Brown and no one else. This forensic evidence proves that Brown was moving forward towards Officer Wilson prior to the final and fatal shot to his head.

Three separate autopsies were conducted on the body of Michael Brown. The first was conducted by the St. Louis County Medical Examiner's Office. The second was conducted privately on behalf of the Brown family by nationally renowned forensic pathologist Dr. Michael Baden. The third autopsy was conducted by government assigned pathologists at the FBI's request. The findings of all three autopsies were consistent that there were *no* gunshot wounds to Michael Brown's back.

Michael Brown was not reaching for his waistband when shot by Officer Wilson.

False. The statements of nearby witnesses, supported by cell phone video, conclusively prove that Officer Wilson never approached or touched Michael Brown's body after Brown was fatally shot and fell to the street.

Prior to Brown's body being removed from the scene, a SLCME medicolegal investigator photographically documented the position of Brown's body on the pavement. Brown was observed to be on his stomach with his right cheek on the pavement and his buttocks partially raised upwards.

Brown's uninjured left arm was partially bent under his body, with his left hand at his waistband and balled up in a fist. His uninjured right arm was back behind him, almost at his right side, with his injured right hand at hip level, palm up. Brown's shorts were observed to be positioned below his waist and buttocks as if they had partially fallen down.

The positioning of Brown's left hand balled up into a fist proximate to his waistband is consistent with Officer Wilson's statement to investigators that Brown had been reaching into his waistband underneath his shirt when Wilson fired at Brown. The position of Brown's shorts midway below his buttocks is an indication that his shorts may have been falling down as he ran towards Officer Wilson and was fired upon.

"Hands up! Don't shoot!" - Michael Brown had his hands up in surrender when he was shot by Officer Wilson.

False. The autopsy reports, photographs, and diagrams of the bullet strikes to Michael Brown's body and the trajectory of the paths of those bullets through Brown's body do not support allegations that Brown had his hands up in surrender at any time during his confrontation with Officer Wilson before Wilson shot at and killed him. Several of the so-called witnesses interviewed by investigators made statements to this effect that were not supported by the forensic and medical evidence in this incident.

Why didn't Officer Wilson 'tase' Michael Brown? How does a "TASER® work?

A TASER® is an electronic control weapon or "ECW" that many officers carry on their duty belts. The ECW uses electrical energy in the form of voltage, absent amperage, to incapacitate physically threatening, resistant or violent subjects. ECW's are officially classified as "less lethal" defensive weapons in the law enforcement, forensic, legal, and military communities. The most popular ECW used in the law enforcement community is referred to by its acronym "TASER®," which stands for "Thomas A. Swift's Electric Rifle," from the science fiction adventure book series of many years ago. Over 90% of police officers who carry an ECW are armed with the TASER® Model X-26.

Think of an ECW as a computer shaped somewhat like a futuristic handgun that discharges electrical energy which is referred to as "load." When electrical load is correctly introduced into the body, it disrupts the instructions that the brain sends to the muscles and appendages. This causes the muscles and joints in the body to seize up. Subjects who are successfully struck by an ECW's metal probes that carry electrical load experience "gait ataxia" (loss of balance and coordination) and often fall to the ground where officers can swarm and restrain them.

In this case, the question is moot: *Officer Wilson had no TASER® electronic control weapon*, so any speculative "would-a, could-a, should-a" argument that he could have tased Michael Brown to avoid resorting to deadly force is irrelevant. In fact, it is far more likely than not that even if Wilson had been armed with a TASER®, Brown's initial distance from the officer of at least thirty feet would have been out of range of the weapon.

The "reactionary gap"

The relevant concept here is what we in the force training community refer to as the "reactionary gap" – a measurement of the distance between an officer and a running subject compared to the officer's ability to react defensively to the subject's assault. Some use-of-force trainers have referred to this concept as the "21 Foot Rule," indicating a tested distance from which a subject armed with an edged weapon can successfully engage an armed officer and kill him before the officer can successfully shoot and stop the assailant charging forward with deadly intent.

Forensically, given the circumstances of the environment of this encounter - Brown's demonstration of violence and the reactionary gap between officer and subject (as determined by FBI investigators), as well as the existing forensic evidence, including credible witness statements -there is little doubt that if Wilson had not resorted to deadly force, Brown would have been able to overpower and violently assault him.

Using his OC pepper spray chemical agent would have been a poor tactical decision because of the initial distance between Wilson and Brown. When Brown quickly closed the gap between himself and Wilson, hitting the face, which is the only effective target area for this chemical weapon, would have been extremely difficult. Also, the pepper spray more likely than not would have had little to no effect on Brown due to his possible drug influence and the time it would have taken for the spray to work, compared to his ability to quickly close the distance between himself and the officer. Although Officer Wilson did possess his ASP expandable baton, this weapon is designed to be used for very close engagements.

In light of Officer Wilson's knowledge that Brown had already repeatedly punched him and had attempted to disarm and shoot him, it would have been a very dangerous and poor tactical decision for the armed officer to move closer to the violent, crazed, and larger suspect and provide Brown with yet another opportunity to grab onto him and take away his sidearm.

Police officers are taught in their use-of-force and defensive tactics classes that eighty-six percent of officers who struggle with suspects land on the ground, where twenty-five percent of them are seriously injured. And twelve percent are ultimately killed by suspects who are able to overpower them, take away their weapon(s) and kill them with those weapons.

Those are not good odds for the police officer. It should always be kept in mind that police officers are armed, and when they encounter physically threatening, resistive, and/or violent subjects close-up, the officer literally brings his weapons to that subject – weapons that are likely to be used on the officer.

Why couldn't Officer Wilson have used other less lethal weaponry to subdue Michael Brown?

As discussed, the forensic evidence clearly shows that Michael Brown suddenly and violently attacked Officer Wilson when the officer was trapped in the driver's seat of his patrol SUV with the driver's side door closed. In this position, the very confined physical environment of the vehicle's cockpit and the manner of Brown's violent punching attack obstructed and prevented Wilson from accessing his OC pepper spray. Wilson's ASP baton had to be expanded in order to be used, obviously impossible, given the confines of the vehicle's interior.

After Officer Wilson and Brown struggled over control of the pistol and Brown was shot and then fled, Wilson exited his SUV and briefly gave chase. He de-escalated by using his officer presence and verbal skills, repeatedly yelling at Brown to "Stop!" and "Get on the ground!" Witness statements, supported by forensic evidence that corroborate Wilson's account of the encounter, indicate that Brown ignored the officer's repeated commands and then suddenly stopped and faced Wilson. Brown then charged Wilson as the officer began to disengage, while continuing to yell orders to "Stop! Get on the ground!" and pointing his gun at Brown.

The encounter turns deadly.

At this moment, Officer Wilson had unsuccessfully attempted to use officer presence, verbal communication, loud orders, and disengaging in an effort to control the hostile, resistive and violent Brown. Officer

Wilson was already keenly aware that Brown had just violently assaulted him and had attempted to physically disarm and shoot him. Wilson knew that Brown was a significantly larger person and was possibly under the influence of drugs.

He saw Brown reach under his shirt to his concealed waistband with his left hand while moving rapidly towards him and believed Brown to be "goal-oriented" and about to seriously injure or kill him.

Police officer training and federal civil rights case laws that provide guidelines on the use of force, including deadly force, do not require officers under such circumstances to use the "least intrusive level(s) of force" to stop an imminent threat of serious bodily injury or death. The courts state only that any quanta of force an officer uses for self-defense, defense of others, or capture must only be "objectively reasonable," given the "totality of circumstances."[13]

In this case, Brown was out of range for Officer Wilson to use his OC pepper spray, which would not have been the proper selection against a very large, possibly drug influenced subject who had just attempted to disarm and shoot the officer and was rapidly re-engaging him. It would also have been inappropriate and extremely dangerous for Officer Wilson to have attempted to expand and use his ASP baton because this would have forced Wilson to come into extremely close striking contact with Brown, who had already demonstrated his ability and commitment to disarm and attack the officer.

Given the "totality of circumstances" Officer Wilson was faced with in his confrontation with Brown and his belief that Brown was reaching into a concealed area of his waistband to possibly produce a deadly weapon, Wilson's use of his handgun was reasonable and consistent with the "standard of care" in officer safety and use-of-force tactics in which officers are trained.

---

[13] Case cite: Graham v. Connor, 490 U.S. 386, 396-397, 109 S. Ct (1989)

Officer Wilson was a problematic officer who had a number of citizen complaints prior to this incident and was prone to use force excessively.

False. Federal prosecutors were aware of and investigated prior complaints against Officer Wilson, as well as media reports alleging that Wilson had engaged in misconduct. None of these so-called complaints or allegations were ever substantiated.

Summary: crime and race

The "Ferguson Incident" - an officer shooting a felony strong-arm robbery suspect and police assailant - was indeed a tragic set of circumstances for all involved. Everyone should remember that the Black Lives Matter leaders, members, other black activists, and the mainstream media created the narrative that Officer Wilson had shot and killed "an unarmed teenager." While it is true that Michael Brown was eighteen years old when he died, he was actually – both chronologically and physically - an adult. Further, whereas it is an objective fact that Brown was not in possession of a weapon when Officer Wilson shot and killed him, the true and forensic facts are that Brown had initially violently assaulted and attempted to wrest control of Officer Wilson's gun in an attempt to kill him.

Readers should understand that just because a person has no *physical* weapon in his possession does not at all mean that he does not pose an imminent, lethal threat to a police officer.

Despite the politically charged atmosphere by racial activists, fueled by an uninformed, biased news media and irresponsible members of the Black Lives Matter movement, this officer-involved shooting incident was correctly and objectively investigated by local, state and federal investigators and prosecutors, as well as the St. Louis County Grand Jury.

My opinion, supported by FBI and local investigators, USDOJ prosecutors and the St. Louis County Grand Jury, is that at the time that Officer Wilson shot and killed Michael Brown, Brown did in fact pose a significant, reasonable imminent threat of serious bodily injury or death to Officer Wilson.

In the end, Officer Wilson was seen to have acted in an objectively reasonable manner when he was forced to shoot and kill Brown, and no criminal charges were brought against him. However, the political pressures and the emotional and psychological trauma that Wilson undoubtedly experienced caused him to resign from the Ferguson Police Department. A good officer lost his job, perhaps forever estranged from a career he cherished. And the Brown family lost a son whom they were ultimately unable to control.

As I will emphasize throughout this book, racial activists, including the radical and revolutionary Black Lives Matter movement and its surrogates, took full advantage of the Ferguson incident. They lost no time immediately descending upon the town of Ferguson, chanting false narrative slogans such as *"Hands up! Don't shoot!"* which was born out of the shooting of Michael Brown.

BLM members and other radical groups marched in the streets of Ferguson and across this nation under this false banner violently engaging police, spewing racial hatred and polarizing the white, minority and law enforcement communities.

Of all the alleged victims of violations of black civil rights by law enforcement, the BLM leaders chose an almost 300-pound, out-of-control, possibly drug influenced, intimidating, violent young felon and thug as the poster child for their movement - a movement largely predicated upon the fictitious "Hands up! Don't shoot!"

As an aside, very few people know that before Officer Darren Wilson responded to the scene of his now infamous encounter with Michael Brown, now referred to as the "Ferguson Incident," he had been engaged in providing emergency medical care to a two-year old possible black toddler who was experiencing breathing difficulties at the

Northwinds Apartment Complex in Ferguson. Officer Wilson heard the radio call broadcast regarding the theft from the Ferguson Market. However, instead of immediately responding, he elected to remain with the distraught mother until health care workers arrived on-scene before leaving. Officer Wilson was no racist; he was a lifesaver who was committed to public service and the citizens of Ferguson.

You now know the real facts and forensic evidence behind this extremely controversial incident. It should come as no surprise that a political movement bases its origin on a fable. Time and again, entire nations have gone to war over incidents that did not happen. But, as we will see throughout this book, repetition of the narrative of a crime that fits the political biases of its creators should cause us to be highly skeptical and to ask what, if any, insights forensic science can bring to the case.

That's what this book is about. It is a continual reminder that, as Mark Twain said, "What gets us into trouble is not what we don't know. It's what we know for sure that just ain't so."

Chapter 4

The Who, What and Where – and the real goals - of the Black Lives Matter Movement

The Who

As we learned in Chapter 1, the Black Lives Matter (BLM) movement was founded in 2013, by three radical, gay women, Angela Garza, Patrisse Cullors and Opal Tometi. Both Garza and Cullors have their roots in the uber-liberal Bay Area cities of San Francisco and Oakland, CA, while Tometi hails from New York City.

Alicia Garza

Ms. Garza, a co-founder and chief ranking administrative officer of the BLM movement, is also employed as the Special Projects Director and spokesperson for the National Domestic Workers Alliance, a political labor and domestic workers advocacy organization with chapters in Atlanta, GA and the San Francisco Bay Area. Garza has also held positions as the Executive Director of another workers advocacy organization, People Organized to Win Employment Rights (POWER), and as a street organizer for Just Cause, which describes itself as a low-income, multi-racial tenant advocacy organization, based in Oakland, CA.

Ms. Garza is a well-educated and openly gay single woman. She received her BA in Anthropology and Sociology from the University of California – San Diego (2002) and obtained a Master's degree in Ethnic Studies from San Francisco State University (2009). Garza received a

"Best of the Bay Area – Local Hero" award in 2008 from the LGBT community newspaper *The San Francisco Bay Guardian*. [14]

From all accounts, including excerpts from speeches and interviews Alicia Garza has provided to various media outlets, she favors a Marxist political ideology. Garza states that she is inspired by and looks up to Marxist radical and revolutionary figures from the Sixties and Seventies, such as former Black Panther Party members Assata Shakur and Angela Davis. She also admires and has followed the teachings of Ella Baker, a civil rights organizer who supported socialism and the Communist Party in the 1930's; Audre Lorde, a black Marxist lesbian feminist; and the radical and violent Weather Underground.

Garza's admiration for Assata Shakur, aka JoAnne Chesimard, as a personal role model is profound. For those who may not know or recall, Shakur is a black revolutionary activist and a former member of the Black Panther Party and the Black Liberation Army between 1971 and 1973. She was convicted of murdering New Jersey State Trooper Werner Foerster and seriously wounding Trooper James Harper during a vehicle stop in May, 1973. Shakur escaped from prison in 1979 and fled to Cuba, where she received political asylum from the communist Castro government and remains in exile. [15]

Ms. Garza describes the BLM movement as "an opportunity for black folks to come together to love each other, to celebrate our resilience in the face of adversity - but also to come together to organize and to build a social, political and economic power to change our conditions." She often speaks out on what she refers to as "white supremacist domination" and asserts that blacks are "uniquely, systematically, and savagely targeted by the State."

Garza states that she is "deeply committed to the liberation of black people" and refers to law enforcement encounters with members of the

---

[14] http://www.linkedin.com/profile/AliciaGarza

[15] https://en.wikipedia.org/wiki/Assata_Shakur

black community in terms of "black oppression," "police violence" and "police terrorism." She believes and states that "Police violence is the tip of the iceberg when it relates to the conditions overall of black people across the globe."

Patrisse Cullors

Co-founder Patrisse Cullors describes herself as an artist, a community organizer, and a freedom fighter. She says that her commitment to her work "was shaped by a history of witnessing state violence." Cullors describes being raised as a young gay woman in a low-income, heavily policed barrio neighborhood in Van Nuys, CA during the wars on drugs and gangs in the 1990's.

When Cullors "came out" as a gay black woman, she was kicked out of her home and self-raised with other gay black women her age who befriended her. Her biological father spent most of his adult life in prison, only to die months after his release in 2009. Her brother was incarcerated in the L.A. County jail system at 19. She alleges that while in jail, the deputies "beat and tortured him." There is no evidence to confirm her assertion.

Cullors says that it was her early familiarity with the criminal justice system, watching black teens and young men being stopped and frisked on the street and arrested and incarcerated in large numbers, that eventually formed the center of her rage and her understanding of the world. [16], [17]

Before becoming involved in the BLM movement, Cullors founded Dignity and Power Now, an organization that she says is "dedicated to protecting incarcerated people and their families" in the Los Angeles area. Ms. Cullors is also invested in her role as "Truth and Reinvestment

---

[16] http://www.facebook.com/pages/patrisse-cullors

[17] Interview of Patrisse Cullors by Michael Segalov, *Vice UK*, p. 1

Campaign Director" at the Ella Baker Center for Human Rights in Oakland, CA, where she works as an organizer with communities she defines as being affected "by state and law enforcement violence." In this capacity, she teaches disenfranchised communities to respond in a rapid and coordinated way through the creation of an online support network, toolkits, and a registry of local and national resources.[18]

In 2013, it was Cullors who used a hashtag (#) in front of friend and BLM co-founder Alicia Garza's poignant letter to friends on her Facebook page that "#Blacklivesmatter." And the social-media-savvy BLM co-founder, Opal Tometi, director of the Black Alliance for Just Immigration, posted the phrase on multiple social media accounts, pleading for support. The actions of these two individuals catapulted the "Black Lives Matter" sentiment into a multinational movement in 2014, following the Michael Brown/Darren Wilson shooting incident in Ferguson, Missouri.[19]

Like her co-founders, Patrisse Cullors is a well-educated and socially networked radical community organizer who appears to be a true believer in the political ideology that a "white supremacist"-based state government is responsible for the systematic oppression and incarceration of blacks and the use of law enforcement lackeys to accomplish this objective.

She firmly believes - and has stated - that black women "are leading and are the architects of the [BLM] movement." According to Cullors, black women have historically led other important black movements. She points to Ella Baker, Diane Nash, and Fannie Lou Hamer as notable radical black women who were critical in developing those movements. Cullors sees the future of black women in movements like BLM as

---

[18] http://ellabakercenter.org/about/staff-and-board/partisse-cullors

[19] http://www.politico.com/magazine/politico50/2015/alicia-garza-patrisse-cullors-opal-tometi

"being on the front lines, strategizing, organizing and developing policies in Ferguson, MO and around the country."[20]

Patrisse Cullors' history as an active, radical community organizer is well documented. While a relatively young woman, she has, at the time of this writing, been involved in organizing groups and communities for over eleven years. Cullers' organizing experience includes the Labor Community Strategy Center's Community Rights Campaign. This group seeks to decriminalize truancy and amend the Los Angeles daytime curfew laws, while also raising money for the grassroots human/civil rights Dignity and Power Now, or "DPN."

DPN fights to expand the rights of incarcerated prisoners and their families in Los Angeles County. It also hosts another prisoner advocacy group, the Coalition to End Sheriff's Violence in L.A. Jails. Ms. Cullers' organizing efforts continue to produce informational workshops and to push for more accountability and transparency in the Los Angeles County Sheriff's Department's treatment of prisoners.

As I explain below, Cullors and her BLM movement co-founders are currently involved in developing and advancing legislation that will see severe reductions in law enforcement funding and redistribution of those monies to fund additional entitlement programs in poor communities; the creation of citizen bodies that independently investigate uses of police force; and the eventual degradation of the Peace Officers' Bill of Rights.[21]

Opal Tometi

Opal Tometi is the third co-founder of the Black Lives Matter movement. An openly gay woman, Tometi is a black feminist writer,

---

[20] Ibid., http://ellabakercenter.org/about/staff-and-board/partisse-cullors

[21] Ibid., Interview of Patrisse Cullors by Michael Segalov, *Vice UK*, p. 4

who alternately describes herself as an "American activist," a "communications strategist," and a "cultural organizer."

She is currently the executive director of one of the country's leading black organizations for immigrant rights, referred to as the "Black Alliance of Just Immigration" (BAJI). The BAJI, as described on its website, is "a national organization that educates and advocates to [*sic*] further immigration rights and racial justice together with African-American, Afro-Latino, and Caribbean immigrant communities." In this position, Tometi networks and collaborates with communities in Oakland, Los Angeles, Phoenix, New York, and several Southern states.

Like her co-founder sisters, Tometi is an educated woman who holds a Bachelor of Arts degree in History and a Masters of Arts degree in Communication and Advocacy. She is the daughter of Nigerian immigrants and grew up in Phoenix, Arizona, where she is on the board of the Puente Movement. The family immigrated to the United States in 1983. Tometi currently resides in New York City.

Tometi recalls reading BLM movement co-founder Alicia Garza's Facebook post about the shooting deaths of Trayvon Martin and Michael Brown. Garza wrote that "Black Lives Matter" and called for members of the Black community to band together to fight injustice. Tometi states that Garza's "rallying call" immediately resonated with her.

She believes that the BLM movement has to be broad enough to capture the state of black life, including the fact that blacks are experiencing a culture of violence that they need to be able to address. She recalls walking with a friend out of the Fruitvale Station (Oakland, CA) when they heard the news that George Zimmerman, the private citizen who shot and killed Trayvon Martin, had been acquitted by a jury in Florida.

Tometi says that "although justice would have been finding [Zimmerman] guilty," she knew that she and others could not sit still with their feelings of hopelessness and that she needed to be involved in a movement and be committed to a cause. Tometi found her cause to be community organizing.

Tometi sees the BLM movement not only as an affirmation for black people, but also as a demand "because the system was not designed for justice for [blacks]." She believes that "It is really important that we establish a really broad notion of who is Black America."

Tometi envisions the BLM movement as a liberation movement for the black people, one that will break down the current criminal justice structures that oppress blacks. For Tometi, "The reality is that we deserve to live in a world where we are not murdered. We deserve to live in a world where there is no impunity; but beyond this question of impunity there are all of these structures that are actually doing a disservice to our people." She identifies these "structures" as the immigration, education, health care, criminal justice, and court systems.

According to Tometi, "Extreme poverty, wealth, and war are linked to extreme policing of bodies and borders." She identifies global issues and policies such as the North American Free Trade Agreement (NAFTA) and the Trans-Pacific Partnership as Black Lives Matter issues.

The "Where": BLM reaches far beyond Ferguson.

Here is where the reach of the BLM movement extends far beyond Ferguson, MO. Indeed, the BLM movement is not even restricted to national issues such as alleged human and civil rights abuses by the American law enforcement and criminal justice communities against the black community. *The BLM movement's interests and designs are international in scope. Those who think otherwise are simply uninformed and naïve.*

Tometi describes black communities as being "gutted." She identifies the culprits of this destabilization as the police, the institutionalization of young black men and women, an anti-immigration posture, dissolving health care and education systems," and "state sanctioned violence." She says, "My hope is that our people will be able to pivot and understand the various ways they are experiencing this violence and we will continue to rise up and fight back."

Since Tometi is an avowed lesbian, she is concerned about what she refers to as the "lack of inclusivity of trans-gender and queer women" in the discussion of human rights. Without providing any evidence, research, or vetted statistical data to support her allegations, Tometi repeatedly refers to what she describes as "almost a death a week among trans-gender women in 2015." However, even she concedes that "those deaths don't fit so neatly into what we understand as the Black Lives Matter movement in that they aren't so clearly connected to state violence."

So what, then, is the nexus between what Tometi refers to as "state sponsored violence" and the death of trans-gender women? Are these homicides? Suicides? Health-related deaths? What local, state or federal systems or institutions are responsible for these so-called deaths? Tometi doesn't tell us; she just tosses this inflammatory allegation out there for public consumption, emotional impact, and outrage. This type of emotional, non-fact-based rhetoric is the hallmark and constant theme of the BLM movement.

Targeting people of color?

Tometi is lock-step in line with BLM movement co-founders Alicia Garza and Patrisse Cullors in her commitment to the belief that the United States government is invested in the "criminalization of people of color." In a recent interview for "The War and Peace Report" on the cable news program "Democracy Now!" Tometi told reporter Amy Goodman,

> *"Yes, the reality is that the criminalization of people of color is impacting us, whether you're a citizen of the United States or not. And what we are seeing right now is the mass criminalization that is leaving low-income people of color, immigrant communities, whether you have permanent resident*

status, whether you're undocumented; and it's leaving them particularly vulnerable to the victims of law enforcement and Immigration and Customs Enforcement.

What we are seeing now is the deputizing of local law enforcement officials, so police, sheriffs, and so on are given the authority to act as though they are ICE agents. And so, this leads to all sorts of mishandling of cases of folks who might be in or out of status in this country. And that we are seeing this collusion between Immigration and Customs Enforcement and local law enforcement is causing rampant immigration and deportation. So the vast numbers that we're seeing, the growing numbers every day; we're seeing thousands and thousands of people each week being deported. This is a result of our immigration and criminal justice systems being intertwined."

Tometi told reporter Goodman that she is recruiting into the BLM movement people "[who] can deliver on a racial justice agenda that incorporates the needs of black immigrants from the Caribbean, Africa, various countries in Latin America and so on."

One has to keep in mind Tometi's own immigrant background and her very focused pro-immigrant position, regardless of whether those immigrants are entering the United States legally or illegally. She is a complete wide-open-border advocate. That is certainly not something that resonates with law enforcement or the vast majority of Americans, including the majority of legal citizens in the black and Hispanic communities.

One component of Opal Tometi's personal design for the BLM movement's future is her description of what she refers to as the "Safety Beyond Policing Network," which she says is focusing on the root causes of the institutionalized diminishing of the black community such as the "policing and criminalizing of poverty." This is the popular Marxist language of the Russian communist leader Vladimir Lenin in the post-World War I era of the 1920's-30's at the time of the Russian Revolution and the rise of communism.

Melina Abdullah – BLM Movement Surrogate

The BLM movement has a number of high-profile surrogates whose job it is to advance the goals, objectives and message of the movement. Professor Melina Abdullah, Ph.D. is certainly one of these. She identifies herself as being on the "Leadership Team" of the movement.

Dr. Abdullah is a professor and the Chair of Pan-African Studies at California State University, Los Angeles. She is also the current Chair for the Council for Affirmative Action for the university's Faculty Association, which is also the faculty's collective bargaining union.

Dr. Abdullah is well connected within the black community. She is known as a community organizer and is a frequent guest on Southern California radio and co-produces and hosts a weekly radio program called "Beautiful Struggle." She uses the Internet to stream worldwide.

Abdullah lists her areas of specialization as "activism and movement building, black politics, black women and 'womanism,' and hip-hop culture." She writes a blog at www.docmellymel.com. Unlike her lesbian BLM movement co-founders, Abdullah is straight and the mother of three children. She resides in Los Angeles, CA.

Dr. Abdullah completed her doctorate in Political Science from the University of Southern California. She received a Bachelor's degree in African-American Studies from Howard University. In 2014, she was appointed to the Los Angeles County Human Relations Commission and is considered by many to be an expert on race relations.

She describes herself as a "womanist scholar-activist" and states that her work "is intrinsically linked to the broader struggles for the liberation of oppressed people." In her online professional profile posted on the CSULA website, Dr. Abdullah openly declares that she is "committed to ending state-sponsored and police violence towards all people – especially black people." [22] However, in the taped lectures and interviews I have reviewed, she is quite vague as to how "the state"

_____

[22] http://web.calstatela.edu/academic/pas/Abdullah.ph.p

sponsors, enables, or ratifies violence, including "police violence" against blacks.

The use of inflammatory accusations without substantiation, one of the mainstays of effective propaganda, is characteristic of the BLM movement. One might repeatedly ask, "*Where exactly is the hard evidence* – recordings, memos, videos, and minutes of secret meetings - of this supposed conspiracy?"

Dr. Abdullah describes herself as "being particularly active in the resistance movement" that has surfaced following the deaths of Oscar Grant (Oakland, CA), Trayvon Martin (Sanford, FL) and Michael Brown (Ferguson, MO). Like her radical and racially-oriented BLM movement co-founders and other Black Nationalist activists, Abdullah's advocacy appears to be focused strictly on the black community. In the very recent past, she publically assailed the uber-liberal and minority community supportive Mayor of Los Angeles Mayor Eric Garcetti during a community meeting, when Garcetti told those assembled that "All lives matter." In a vociferous response, Abdullah openly chastised the mayor, stating,

> "*The mayor has neglected, disrespected and abused the black community for far too long. If you say that all lives matter, you write people out of history. You write slavery out of history.*"[23]

During another meeting before the City of Los Angeles Police Commission, Abdullah openly chastised the commission's Executive Director Richard Tefank and commission members when she called the LAPD "the most murderous department in the country" and then condescendingly told Director Tefank to "Read a book. Read a report!"

Of course, Dr. Abdullah never suggested exactly what book or report the Police Commissioner should read. Abdullah became even more vocal

---

[23] http://www.theblaze.com/stories/2015/10/20/Black-lives-matter-protestors-rush-a-mayors-podium-at-town-hall-watch-what-happens-as-hes-escorted-out-for-safety/

during the meeting, suggesting that commission member and attorney Matthew Johnson who is black, was a "huge donor" to Mayor Garcetti's campaign and was a political appointee who was "divorced and isolated from the black community," and did not represent the interests of black people. In response, Mr. Johnson warned Abdullah that she was being disruptive and then called a recess in order to restore order. When the meeting resumed, Abdullah was refused re-entry to make further comments.

It is interesting to note that Mr. Najee Ali, Reverend Al Sharpton's political director for his L.A. Chapter of the National Action, had personally attended the Police Commission meeting to congratulate attorney Matthew Johnson on his appointment to the LAPD Police Commission. Mr. Ali had just come from another meeting at Los Angeles City Hall where a number of members representing major civil rights and community organizations and religious leaders had voiced their support for Mr. Johnson's appointment as well. [24]

Summary

Black Lives Matter movement co-founders Alicia Garza, Patrisse Cullors, Opal Tometi, and Melina Abdullah are four strong-minded, well-educated, multi-talented, feminist radical revolutionaries who have joined together to found a movement based upon the ideologies of Black Nationalism, Afrikanism, and the Black Liberation Movement. The language consistently used by the leaders, surrogates, members and supporters of the BLM movement - as evidenced by the emotional political rhetoric used by the movement's leaders and surrogates themselves - is anti-capitalist, anti-democracy, anti-police, anti-rule-of-law, and pro-Marxist and revolutionary.

---

[24] Article, *"Tensions mount at LAPD public meeting,"* National News Reporter Charlene Muhammad, 09-30-15

The BLM movement is founded upon a number of false narratives expressed by the co-founders and their surrogates. These tropes, repeated over and over, are "state sponsored violence" against members of the black community and immigrants of color; oppression of black and other immigrants of color; the criminalization of poverty; and the disproportionate, extra-judicial murder of young black men by police.

The designs, goals and objectives of the BLM movement, as expressed by the movement's co-founders in their own words, are not simply national; they are global. Like the movement itself, BLM co-founders and surrogates Alicia Garza, Patrisse Cullors, Opal Tometi and Melina Abdullah, are intelligent, well-connected, social-media-savvy, committed adversaries, who administer a well-funded, organized, and logistically sophisticated and internationally based revolutionary movement.

Attention should be paid to the countries the BLM movement's founders have visited - Palestine, Northern Ireland, Africa - all of which are hotbeds of anti-government revolution that underscore the founders' and movement's future designs.

One might quite justifiably ask, "What does a nationally based black advocacy movement, steeped in pro-Marxist revolutionary language, following the path of previous and current violent Black Nationalist and revolutionary movements, have to do with what is happening in Palestine, Africa and Northern Ireland?" How does visiting those countries move the black community in the U.S. forward? What does visiting revolutionary strongholds in Palestine have to do with the theme "Black Lives Matter?"

And further: Observers of the BLM movement, including the media and politicians, need to ask, loudly and repeatedly, "Exactly how do the false narratives of the BLM movement and the inflammatory, racially polarizing, anti-police, anti-government rhetoric of its founders bring the races, law enforcement and our governments closer together to enhance racial understanding and mutual cooperation? If they don't, then what is the ultimate purpose of this movement and its founders?"

Finally, observers, politicians and the news media owe a responsibility to the American people and the minority community to research and better vet the founders, surrogates, supporters, foundation platform, goals, objectives, and funding sources of the Black Lives Matter movement. They then need to decide whether this radical, Marxist-style and revolutionary organization benefits or undermines the relationship among our nation's diverse peoples - and whether the movement and its supporters ultimately seek to enhance or destroy the American democratic system, our rule of law, and our way of life.

References

http://www.domesticworkers.org

http://www.cjjc.org/

http://www.linkedin.com/profile/AliciaGarza

http://web.calstatela.edu/academic/pas/Abdullah.ph.p

http://socialistworker.org/2003-2/474/474_09_EllaBaker.shtml

http://dignityandpowernow.org

http://www.prisonerswithchildren.org/our-projects/allofus-or-none/

http://www.theblaze.com/stories/2015/10/20/Black-lives-matter-protestors-rush-a-mayors-podium-at-town-hall-watch-what-happens-as-hes-escorted-out-for-safety/

http://www.finalcall.com/artman/publish/National_News2/article_102631.shtml

Chapter 5

Hijacked ideals and the breakdown of society

Make no mistake about it - and I can personally attest as a police consultant who has designed policing programs outside of the United States - Americans have by far the best policing system and some of the best trained officers in the world. At the same time, I also acknowledge that when I visit certain parts of our country, I am stupefied at the lack of progressive training our officers receive. This is not a "police problem;" it is a municipal government problem.

The successes and failures of police training

My professional experience as a retired law enforcement officer and police trainer, and that of the vast majority of law enforcement officers, supervisors, and administrators I speak with, is that officers always want to receive better training so they can do their jobs better. Police officers belong to more organizations that provide training than attorneys; many officers pay out of their own pockets for advanced training beyond what their agencies provide; and many officers are more well-read on the complex subjects of their profession than the vast majority of attorneys, reporters, and community activists who criticize them are in their own professions.

That said, I am consistently disappointed with the lack of funding for progressive law enforcement training. In literally every police practices civil litigation and criminal case I have ever investigated and analyzed, I have found that the key mistakes that the involved officers(s) made was a direct consequence of being improperly trained, or even having no training at all in the issue or problem that ultimately was central to the incident. Therefore, when attorneys, community activists, or members of the Black Lives Matter movement criticize police for not being properly trained, there are occasions when they are correct.

I have very strong feelings about the need for correct, relevant, and progressive training within the law enforcement community. I also believe that if a municipality cannot afford to properly train, equip, and entrust its officers to handle the rigors of a very challenging and difficult policing mission, then it has absolutely no business having a police department and should contract with the local sheriff's department to police the community.

In America's ever evolving society, police who are considered to be "first responders" are increasingly challenged by a host of problems they are undertrained to deal with. Among the most difficult and troublesome circumstances are people experiencing psycho-medical emergencies and synthetic drug influence; suicidality; domestic violence; street gangs; major disturbances; and an increasingly violent and armed society. There is simply no excuse or justification for not training officers properly to deal with the unique difficulties, challenges, and stressors of police work.

When to detain, search, or arrest?

Another one of the messages of the BLM movement is that police officers upon occasion unlawfully stop/detain, search and arrest blacks. In this allegation, they are not entirely incorrect. However, I have found that the truth is (1) *this problem is not unique to blacks; and (2) this is a training issue, rather than a racial bias or racial profiling problem.*

I have encountered a number of police officers and administrators who, when asked or deposed, could not clearly articulate or make a distinction between a subjective and objective standard of proof. That's a problem.

One case I clearly recall involved a former Deputy Chief of the patrol division of the largest urban sheriff's department in the U.S. He was insistent, during his deposition, that "reasonable suspicion" and "probable cause" were the same thing.

They are obviously not. For the lay reader, "reasonable suspicion," is what is objectively required to stop, detain and perhaps search a subject for the presence of a weapon, whereas "probable cause" is what is required to obtain a search warrant or make an arrest, because the officer has objective evidence that a crime has been or is being committed.

These are _significant_ differences in objective standards of proof, and failure to make the proper judgment directly results in unlawful detentions and arrests and illegal searches and seizures.

While members of the BLM movement and other racial activists are quick to allege racial bias or bigotry in "stop and frisk" enforcement actions, this allegation is more an aberration and unsubstantiated speculation than an objective fact.

Even the President can't get it right.

Consider the detention and arrest of Harvard Professor Henry Louis Gates, which I discuss in detail below. Even President Obama, a former professor of Constitutional law, opined that Officer Crowley had no right to stop, detain and subsequently arrest Professor Gates. Obama was completely wrong in his basic understanding of simple laws of detention, arrest and search and seizure. By the way, he was also wrong on the legal and self-defense issues surrounding the Trayvon Martin and Wilson/Brown shooting cases.

If a former university Constitutional law professor and sitting President of the United States is blatantly incorrect in his considered assessment of what I refer to as "Basic Police 101" issues of detention, arrest, police use of force, and civilian self-defense, then why does the general public and the media pour criticism on police when they occasionally err?

My point is that it is entirely reasonable for the public to expect police officers to understand the basic protocols governing arrest, search/seizure, and the use of force. However, it is a completely different subject when angry citizens throw down the race card and allege that police stop/detain and arrest only blacks.

It's not just black citizens. I see this problem across the entire racial spectrum. Again, it's a training issue, not a racial profiling problem.

It is also a valid complaint to allege in certain instances that police have used force, including deadly force, unreasonably and excessively, upon members of the black community. I, along with my firm's multidisciplinary Forensic Death Investigations Team members, have been retained and have successfully investigated, analyzed, and opined in a number of plaintiff and criminal cases against police officers who were ultimately found by triers of fact to have committed such violations.

Recently, we have been witness to controversial fatal police shootings and in-custody deaths in Chicago, Newark, North Charleston, and Baltimore. However, to put this back into context, such cases overall are aberrations and in no way represent the overwhelming, vast number of law enforcement officers who encounter blacks and other minorities for the purpose of enforcement actions. (In Chapter 8, I statistically analyze the false allegation that police shoot and kill a disproportionate number of black men.)

All citizens deserve a quality, well-educated police force protecting them. They deserve to have members of their police forces understand their special needs, challenges, and problems. The municipal governments and law enforcement communities owe this to all citizens.

Why are police distrusted and hated?

Let's keep all of this in perspective. The overwhelming majority of the black community supports law enforcement and truly understands the unique challenges and life risks they face on a daily basis within their community. After all, in some communities, these citizens are hostages in their homes as a direct result of violent crime.

The good, law abiding, and innocent men, women, families, and senior citizens know that police have not created the historic problems of the black community; they merely *respond* to them. In the vast majority of cases, it is the good people who *call* the police to deal with the bad people.

Some members of the minority community - and the black community in particular - have held an historic distrust for law enforcement for several generations. Times of distrust, dislike, and even hatred have surfaced during the civil rights era; the Detroit, New York, and Newark riots; and the Rodney King incident, just to name a few.

The law enforcement community by and large has responded by enhancing its selection process, racially diversifying, increasing education criteria, and developing and implementing diversity, anti-racial-profiling, conflict resolution, use of force, and community policing programs nationwide. A number of cities have instituted Citizen Review Boards and Inspector General Offices to provide police oversight as well.

If someone from outside of the United States were to watch television news programs produced here, he might think that in many parts of the nation, the polarization between the black and law enforcement communities has not decreased since the days of racial strife during the 1950's–1960's. Today, by and large, the leaders and supporters of the Black Lives Matter movement, their politically exploitive surrogates, and an under-informed and/or biased mainstream media are in large part responsible for this continuing distrust of and resistance to police authority.

My personal opinion is that President Obama and former U.S. Attorney General Eric Holder, through their biased and uninformed remarks, have actually widened the chasm between the black and law enforcement communities. Presently, Presidential candidates Hillary Clinton and Bernie Sanders have met with BLM movement leaders and have adopted several of their suggestions for a "new policing plan" without vetting the plan or its intended consequences to the law enforcement and criminal justice communities. (See Chapter 11.)

A close look at the foundations of the BLM movement shows that rather than bringing forward, frank and sincere concerns about incidents of police malpractice and working cooperatively with police and municipal governments to effect change, the leaders of the movement have chosen instead to base their platform upon narratives that are not only objectively and scientifically false, but outrageously so.

BLM movement goals, objectives, and mission of anarchy

Simple research into the backgrounds of the founding members of the BLM movement shows that the leaders all follow the philosophies, ideologies, goals and objectives of militant, radical and violent anti-police, anti-government, Black Nationalist, Afrikaner, Marxist groups and political organizations. The language consistently used by BLM co-founders Alicia Garza, Patrisse Cullors, Opal Tometi and others like Melina Abdullah are replete with the Marxist language of the "oppressed masses" and what they refer to as "state-sponsored violence."

If you read the treatises, articles, and transcripts of recorded interviews and watch video interviews of the BLM leaders, it becomes abundantly clear that *they have absolutely no intention of ever working with the law enforcement to bring about positive change that would ultimately benefit the black community.* That was not their goal when the organization was founded, is not their goal presently, and will never be their goal for the future.

The BLM movement leaders have also been quite clear that this is a "black only" radical movement. They have clearly stated in video recorded interviews that they are not at all interested in working with the non-black communities in advocating for better relations between their movement and government and law enforcement officials. This design is completely consistent with their Black Nationalist and Afrikaner ideology.

As the leaders of the Black Lives Matter movement have amply articulated, their ultimate goals are the disarming, disassembly, and defunding of law enforcement; the diminishing of local, State and the Federal government; and the eventual diminishing of our nation's democratic rule of law. Obviously such measures would result in complete anarchy.

Political disruption and media manipulation

The BLM movement's master battle plan involves the complete disruption of the democratic process. We have already seen evidence of this on the 2016 Presidential campaign trail in the summer of 2015, when BLM movement members took over the assembly room where Democratic/Socialist candidate Bernie Sanders was giving a speech.

As of this writing, leaders of the movement have repeatedly threatened to protest and create havoc to disrupt the upcoming Republican Convention in Cleveland, OH from July 18–21, 2016. They know that Cleveland and regional police agencies will be out in force, and the convention will be reported by national and international news media. There will be even more attention, if that's possible, if the controversial Donald Trump becomes the Republican nominee.

The leaders of the BLM movement understand that Cleveland, which has been Ground Zero for the Officer Michael Brelo murder acquittal and the justified officer-involved fatal shooting of Tamir Rice, will provide a unique opportunity for them to clash with police and disrupt the entire convention, while at the same time garnering 24/7 national and international news coverage.

Remaining on page one of the news each day is an important component in spreading their anti-police, anti-government, Marxist propaganda, and the American public and the international community will have front-row seats for the entire show.

Massaging potential political surrogates

The BLM movement has been diligently cultivating Democratic Presidential candidate Hillary Clinton, so that she will voice support for the movement. They know that Clinton needs the black vote if she has any shot at the Presidency.

The former Secretary of State, who already is the "person of interest" in a federal criminal investigation by 150 FBI agents involving her unsecure personal email server and the possible distribution of numerous highly classified State Department and intelligence documents, has demonstrated that she is willing to do anything to get elected. Ms. Clinton has already met with BLM movement leaders and to date has made a number of statements that show that her rhetoric regarding police and the black community resonate more with the BLM movement than the law enforcement community.

When national Black leaders criticize - but don't lead

President Barack Obama is an excellent example of prominent national black leaders who spend more time criticizing police than leading our nation to solidarity and cooperation between the races and the law enforcement community.

Although Obama has the right to weigh in on controversial subjects, as he often does, the comments he has made in recent memory on a number of controversial police and citizen involved encounters with black men have been non-objective, speculative, inaccurate and/or inappropriate.

The themes throughout all of our black President's comments are an unabashed advocacy for black suspects and unneeded criticism of the police. In the Trayvon Martin shooting incident, Obama remarked that if he had a son, he might look like Martin.

But would Obama's hypothetical son act as Martin did? As we now know, a Florida jury acquitted private citizen George Zimmerman of murdering Martin, who witnesses testified was on top of Zimmerman and slamming the man's head repeatedly into a concrete sidewalk when Zimmerman was forced to shoot and kill him.

During the controversy surrounding Cambridge Police Sergeant Crowley's detention and arrest of Harvard Professor Henry Louis Gates, which I discuss in detail in Chapter 7, Obama criticized the involved officers for "acting stupidly," without reviewing the facts of the incident or displaying any proper understanding of the laws governing laws of detention/arrest and search and seizure.

When addressing the news media, President Obama said that he was not going to discuss the incident because he had not reviewed all of the facts. However, in his next breath, he did exactly that:

> "The Cambridge police acted stupidly in arresting somebody in his house when there was already proof that they were in their own home. . .There's been a long history in this country of African-Americans and Latinos being stopped by law enforcement disproportionately. . .But I think it's fair to say that any of us would be pretty angry."

After the President initially advised the assembled media that "[he] did not know if race played a factor in the incident," Obama ended his comments to the reporters with the statement that "This incident shows how race remains a factor in this society." [25] Is this political "double-speak," or simple disingenuous and racially biased behavior? You decide.

As we now know, Sergeant Crowley's enforcement actions that day were consistent with the law and codified police practices and the standards of care. Professor Gates was the person in the wrong there.

---

[25] http://www.cnn.com/2009/US/07/22/harvard.gates.interview/

Following the officer-involved fatal shooting of 18-year-old felony strong-arm suspect and police assailant Michael Brown in Ferguson, MO, President Obama expressed his condolences to the Brown family over the loss of their son, consistently referred to Brown by his first name, and then told a gathering of the Congressional Black Caucus in Washington, D.C. on September 28, 2014:

> *"Now I know that the people in this room have long understood, in too many communities a gulf of mistrust exists between local communities and law enforcement. Many men of color feel that they are targeted by law enforcement. Guilty of walking while black. Driving while black. They feel fear, resentment and hopelessness."* [26]

However, since the release of the official USDOJ report formally confirming that Officer Wilson's shooting of Michael Brown was legally justified, we have yet to hear that the President met with the equally traumatized Officer Wilson, who has since left law enforcement, to assuage him in *his* grief and depression.

Finally, President Obama's comments regarding what he observes as the black community's distrust of law enforcement provides support to and enables the movement to spread its false narratives. This is a dangerous position to adopt and exacerbates the already extremely difficult task of law enforcement officers who have to police minority communities.

In speaking at the annual conference of the International Association of Chiefs of Police (IACP) in Chicago this past October, President Obama told the assembled police administrators that the Black Lives Matter movement has highlighted an issue that has been ignored in America.

---

[26] http://www.nbcnews.com/watch/nbc-news/obama-comments-on-michael-brown-shooting-3341

He told the audience:

> *"There is a specific problem that is happening in the African-American community that is not happening in other communities, and that is a legitimate issue that we've got to address. The African-American community is not just making this up. It's not something that's just being politicized. It's real. We as a society, particularly given our history, have got to take this seriously."* [27]

While it is also true that President Obama did make some comments that were generally supportive of law enforcement during the IACP conference, historically it sounded like the President was talking out of both sides of his mouth.

Living in a "race bubble"

The problem I see with some nationally prominent black leaders and the race-baiting activists like Jesse Jackson and Al Sharpton is that they are advocates for race instead of objective facts. When they live inside a "race bubble," all they see and the only context they have is the issue of race.

These so-called leaders ignore, deny, deflect, or redirect the real and obvious causes of violence within the black community and of black relationships with other races and the law enforcement community. There is little to no discussion of teen pregnancies; father abandonment; the dissolving family unit; child abuse and neglect; a serious high school dropout rate of up to 50% in many urban communities; the lack of education and job skills; alcohol and drug abuse; street gangs; a horrendous black-on-black homicide rate; and a disproportionate incarceration rate.

---

[27] http://www.usatoday.com/story/news/politics/2015/10/22/speaking-police-obama-defends-Black-lives-matter-movement/74368552/

It is an objective fact that black youths and men are incarcerated in probation correction facilities and adult jails and prisons throughout the United States at numbers disproportionate to their racial demographics. However, members of the Black Lives Matter movement and other black activists fail to provide context that this is actually because black males commit disproportionate numbers of crimes that caused them to be sentenced to those facilities. This is not "systemic racism;" it is simple socio-criminology that is directly related to the aforementioned problems that are historic challenges in other minority communities.

All of these problems share a symbiotic relationship with each other. When members of the BLM movement – and all the supporters, black activists, and political surrogates – clamor about the "disproportionate incarceration rate of young black men," they need to understand that although they are factually correct, there are many reasons for the problems I have just listed. These are not the product of race, but of behaviors and poor life decisions.

Today, as any law enforcement, criminal justice or legal professional knows, with plea bargaining, house arrest, lower sentencing, probation, and a variety of local, state and federal diversion programs specifically designed to decrease jail and prison populations, it is actually pretty difficult to end up in jail or prison. In fact, you really have to work hard to get sentenced to jail or prison, unless you seriously injure or kill someone. Unfortunately, the BLM movement leaders and their supporters never want to discuss the main reason for continued high populations of young black men in jail/prison – *high recidivism rates*.

Local jurisdictions, states, and the federal government just don't have the money to incarcerate non-recidivist, non-violent offenders. For example, a review of Freddie Gray's criminal record in Baltimore, MD before his in-custody death, shows that he had been arrested, imprisoned and released over *twenty* times for crimes ranging from theft to drug possession and sales to assault! Now does that say something about our so-called "racist criminal justice system" - or about Freddie Gray's criminal mindset, behavior and *recidivism*? You tell me. It's really not rocket science.

Summary

There are many good reasons why the law enforcement community should work with minority communities to enhance relationships and improve the quality of life for those residing in desperate communities.

Members of the law enforcement community can always learn more from minority communities. They want to demonstrate - and historically have demonstrated - their willingness and commitment to do so. Conversely, members of the minority community need to be equally trained in understanding the unique challenges and difficulties of policing in modern America. Education and building relationship bridges are mutually beneficial to each side.

At the same time, however, members of the black community need to be aware that radical, militant organizations such as the Black Lives Matter movement are not the vehicle they want - or America needs - to move blacks forward toward improving their future in American society.

Blacks need to keep in mind that the BLM movement is not a panacea for black respect and independence. Rather, it is a politically exploitive entity that if allowed to prosper, will severely polarize the races and damage relations with their law enforcement protectors. The BLM movement is not about "building" anything; it is about tearing down and destroying.

One needs to be reminded that it was not the police who looted and burned down black owned businesses in Ferguson, MO and Baltimore, MD. It was members of the BLM movement and other black anarchists. Again, such militant, violent activism harkens back to the days of the Nazi and Fascist movements immediately preceding World War II.

So the ultimate consideration is this: when you are in desperate need of help and your life hangs in the balance in the dead of night, whom would you rather call: members of the BLM movement - or the cops?

Just some more food for thought.

Chapter 6

Following the Money – Who Funds the BLM Movement?

It takes money to fund a national movement whose leaders and members travel nationally and internationally to advance their cause, disrupt the democratic process, and learn new methods of civil protest and revolution to eventually upset the rule of law.

As a police detective who once investigated street gangs and complex economic fraud, I learned a long time ago that if I was going to investigate a goal-oriented group or persons of interest, I needed to "follow the money."

Much can be revealed about a group, if one takes time to investigate its funding sources. You learn how the group's leaders and members derive their income and whether the funding sources are legitimate and legal or not. You can also learn about the end-objectives and beliefs of the funders. This is important because it will more often than not align with those of the funded group and its leaders.

As I have already discussed, it would be a naïve, but understandable mistake to assume or believe that the BLM movement is just a group of disenfranchised, militant agitators and students who have banded together to protest alleged police brutality and violations of black civil rights. While these are certainly components of the movement, there is far more to the BLM's story.

The BLM movement is an organized, sophisticated and well-funded organization bent upon radically changing the American political and democratic landscape on many levels. If you remember Presidential candidate Barack Obama's telling his followers that he was going to "fundamentally change America," and if you now see how this country has been negatively transformed to date, you begin to grasp what "change" means. Change can be good - and change can be very bad. The key is how a group, its leaders, and its funders go about creating that change.

If you scrutinize the BLM movement's funding sources, you can determine more likely than not how an emboldened BLM movement would change our current law enforcement, criminal justice, social service, education and political landscape. My research shows if these changes were to occur, the result would be dangerous, even disastrous for America.

So let's start with the money trail. Here is some interesting information on how the BLM movement is being funded.

The George Soros connection

George Soros is a major funder of the BLM movement, through his foundation, the Open Society Institute. Financial records and media reports document that Soros has given at least $33 million to groups and persons who support his far left political agenda, including BLM-movement-affiliated groups.

Soros, a multi-billionaire and international currency manipulator, is often referred to as "The Godfather of the Left." *Forbes* Magazine lists him as the world's 22nd richest man, worth approximately $22 billion.

Media sources (listed below) have reported that Soros' monetary donations have helped to ferment revolutions. He has undermined various national currencies and funded radicals around the world. He was convicted in France of insider dealing and was fined $3 million; he was also fined an additional $2 million in Hungary. In the United States, Soros' donations have promoted everything from drug legalization to anti-death penalty strategies.

Where Soros' money goes

Soros started his Open Society Institute (OSI) in 1993 as a vehicle for donating to progressive far-left-wing, radical, and militant activists, politicians and groups. The Institute is actually a sophisticated network of international foundations, projects, and partners from over 100 countries.

The list of activists, politicians, groups and radical organizations receiving funding from Soros' Open Society Institute reads like a Who's Who of the progressive and radical left. ACORN, MORE, the National Council of La Raza, The Tides Foundation, Moveon.org, the highly secretive progressive political organization Democracy Alliance, and many others are all funded in some manner by Soros' Open Society Institute.

One of the organizations that Soros provides major funding to is All of Us or None. This political group seeks to change voting laws to allow former and current prison inmates, parolees, and other felons to vote in elections. Another group, the American Friends Service Committee, views the United States as the principal cause of human suffering around the world. This political activist organization favors America's unilateral disarmament; the dissolution of American borders; amnesty for all illegal aliens; the abolition of the death penalty; and the repeal of the Patriot Act.

The Sausalito, CA Tides Foundation, established in 1976 by California activist Drummond Pike, has been set up as a "public charity" that receives money from a variety of secret donors. According to The Tides Foundation website, "We strengthen community-based organizations and the progressive movement by providing an innovative and cost-effective framework for your philanthropy."

The foundation has actually been created as a money-laundering operation that enables secret donors to funnel money to radical groups through "donor advised contributions." This method allows donors to avoid being identified as supporters of radical groups, and it prevents the public documentation of their donations. This more sophisticated scheme allows nonprofit entities to create a vehicle for funneling money to the Tides Foundation as a "for-profit" entity, thereby avoiding state and federal laws that prevent non-profits from funneling monies into their own for-profit businesses.

A radical, far-left agenda

Tides contributes to a number of radical, far left progressive causes. These include: the banning of citizen ownership of firearms; extreme environmentalism; the "exclusion of humans from public and private wildlands"; anti-free trade campaigns; abolition of the death penalty; and others. *Tides* is also a member organization of the International Human Rights Funders Group, a network of more than seventy other similar contribution conduits that finance left-wing groups and causes.

The Soros-funded group The Malcolm X Grassroots Movement has strong ties to the Black Lives Matter movement. This radical, militant, Black Nationalist group views the U.S. as a racist nation that discriminates against blacks.

The Malcolm X Grassroots Movement funded and produced a report entitled *Operation Ghetto Storm*, authored by liberal writer Arlene Eisen, who used pseudo-science to promote the false hashtag slogan, "Every 28 hours a black man is killed by police," which remains a popular chant of BLM movement protesters at anti-police rallies and demonstrations. Ms. Eisen's research was later debunked by this author and other reporters, and she subsequently confessed to blatant factual errors in her so-called "research."

Soros' political contributions to Illinois State Senate candidate Barack Obama started the young Senator's political career. When Obama later announced his run for the Presidency, Soros quickly donated the maximum amount allowed to get Obama into the White House. A number of Soros' left wing organizations and their chief administrators have close ties to President Obama and the White House.

Politically, George Soros could be best described as a far-left socialist progressive. His political objectives appear to be focused on diminishing America's standing internationally as a world power. His actions indicate that he would like to see the U.S. subservient to international bodies such as the World Bank and United Nations. Soros believes and has written that there are collective interests that transcend state boundaries and that the sovereignty of states must be subordinated to international laws and institutions.

Some of the far-left causes and organizations that George Soros financially supports include: The Advancement Project, an organization that facilitates organizing "communities of color" into political units which in turn disseminate leftist world views; America's Voice, an open-borders group promoting "comprehensive immigration reform," including amnesty for illegal aliens; the American Immigration Council, a non-profit open-borders group that supports amnesty for illegal aliens; the American Prospect, Inc., a corporation that educates and mentors leftwing journalists and organizes strategy meetings for leftist leaders; and the Center for Constitutional Rights, a pro-Castro organization that supports an open border agenda, has opposed nearly all post-9/11 anti-terrorism measures by the U.S. government, and suggests that American injustice provokes acts of international terrorism.

While there are literally scores of leftist organizations funded by George Soros and his Open Society Institute, the themes that are consistent in the goals and objectives of the vast majority of his funded groups have been open borders, amnesty for illegal aliens, and the diminishing of the American democratic process, our rule of law, criminal justice system, and Homeland Security protection system.

Soros' money and the BLM movement

A number of groups directly and indirectly tied to the BLM movement have received funding from Soros' Open Society Institute. Here are a few of them and their relationships to left-wing, progressive, and/or radical politics. As you read on, you will see a theme of sorts developing between the BLM movement, radical people and organizations, powerful politicians, and their combined radical objectives for changing American society. Remember – *follow the money.*

One radical political activist organization that has received money from George Soros' Open Society Institute is Missourians Organizing Reform Empowerment (MORE). This organization was formerly known by its more recognizable name, the Association of Community Organizations for Reform Now, or "ACORN." As you may recall, ACORN was involved in a number of nefarious political activities in support of President Obama's previous election campaign. The organization went bankrupt in 2010.

Jeff Ordower, who is the founder of MORE, told the *Huffington Post* that the organization is "focused on climate and justice work." While MORE's objectives appear to be strange bedfellows, they are two of President Obama's major social change objectives for America.

Jeff Ordower has told the *Huffington Post* that he "welcomes those attempting to scale up numbers of radical organizers who can finally support themselves in the work." The *Washington Times*, *Infowars,* and other media outlets document that MORE and Ordower received a substantial donation from Soros' OSI, designed to be paid out for the purpose of retaining and subsidizing professional protestors. The monies were also used for travel logistics such as renting buses and providing food for the activists to travel to Ferguson, MO and Baltimore, MD, where they created civil unrest that ultimately led to the Michael Brown and Freddie Gray riots in those cities.

Another group that has teamed up with MORE is the Organization for Black Struggle (OBS). The OBS, founded in St. Louis in 1980, preaches black liberation, as well as "political empowerment, economic justice and the cultural dignity of the African-American community, especially the black working class."

Recruiting professional protestors

Infowars released the MORE- and OBS-funded ad on social media for "application" for activist protestors. This ad/application referred to a Movement Support Fund, which stated, "The Organization for Black Struggle (OBS) and Missourians Organizing for Reform and Empowerment (MORE) are pleased to offer travel funding for individuals and grassroots groups that are working to advocate for police accountability and black lives."

MORE and OBS Ad for professional protesters

OBS gained some media prominence in Missouri as a result of the group's presence at protests in Ferguson, following the Michael Brown shooting.

The *Washington Times* reported that buses full of activist protestors from Soros-funded groups like the Samuel Dewitt Proctor Conference, the Drug Policy Alliance, Make the Road New York, Equal Justice USA, New York, the Advancement Project, and Center for Community Change (Washington DC) descended on Ferguson, MO in August and remained off and on in the town to protest at City Hall until December, 2015.

The purpose of maintaining a high-profile presence was not only to protest the Michael Brown shooting and alleged discrimination, but also to keep a media spotlight on a number of interrelated causes that the groups advocate on behalf of, such as changing the law enforcement and criminal justice systems; changing drug policies; immigration reform; and government funding of other radical and progressive social programs.

George Soros and MORE's retention and funding of professional protesters have not been without internal strife and controversy. When their retained protesters either did not receive their monthly checks or the organizations stopped funding them, the social media trending hashtag *#CutTheCheck* soon appeared online. *#CutTheCheck* was a social media mechanism that angry protesters used to voice their frustration and anger in not getting paid by their benefactors.

At one point, Millennial Activist United (MAU) co-founder Brittany Ferrell used the group's Facebook account to voice her disapproval by posting a letter to MORE demanding that they "cut the checks" to demonstrators they had retained to protest in Ferguson and Baltimore. The MAU is a black activist group founded by gay black women during the Ferguson protests. The group has been involved in actively protesting and supporting other Ferguson protesters by providing them with food and medical aid.

The Jay-Z and Beyoncé Connection

Among the most high-profile donors to the Black Lives Matter movement are international music celebrities Jay-Z and Beyoncé Carter.

The news and social media, and people directly connected to the couple, have documented that the billionaire hip-hop power couple have donated generously to supporting the movement and bailing radical and militant Ferguson and Baltimore protesters out of jail. It should be remembered that a number of protesters were directly involved in the burning and looting of black-owned and employed businesses in both cities.

Writer and filmmaker Dream Hampton, who authored Jay-Z's memoirs *Decoded*, revealed on her Twitter account on May 17, 2015 that the Carters had wired "tens of thousands of dollars" to the BLM movement for general support and to bail out BLM movement protesters after the Ferguson and Baltimore protests. In fact, Hampton emailed the *New York Daily News* stating, "I can say that I've personally helped facilitate donations [that Jay-Z and Beyoncé have] given to protesters directly and they have never asked for anything in return, especially publicity."

Hampton also tweeted, "When we needed money for bail for the Baltimore protesters, I hit Jay up, as I had for Ferguson; [he] wired tens of thousands in mins."

So what is Hampton's connection to the BLM movement? She is reportedly a member of the radical Malcolm X Grassroots organization. It is entirely possible that Jay-Z and Beyoncé may have been feeling pressure from the BLM movement and its supporting groups because Jay-Z had rapped about the movement, and the couple has been seen wearing clothing inscribed with Black Lives Matter slogans but not donating to the cause. That issue has apparently been rectified.

It is also interesting to note that Ms. Hampton quickly took down her Tweets about Jay-Z and Beyoncé's donations to the BLM movement, while saying that she did not care "if Jay-Z got mad" for her unsolicited posts. However, the cat was already out of the bag when her posts were quickly captured as screenshots that appear here.

dream hampton @dreamhampton

I'm going to tweet this and I don't care if Jay gets mad.

5/17/15, 8:38 AM

63 RETWEETS **18** FAVORITES

 Jada @Jada_D_Snicket 6m
@dreamhampton I knew they were helping. People don't realize that humility and not wanting to detract from the cause is an admirable thing

 dream hampton @dreamhampton

When BLM needed infrastructure money for the many chapters that we're growing like beautiful dandelions, Carters wrote a huge check.

5/17/15, 8:41 AM

88 RETWEETS **24** FAVORITES

 dream hampton @dreamhampton

When we needed money for bail for Baltimore protestors, I asked hit Jay up, as I had for Ferguson, wired tens of thousands in mins.

5/17/15, 8:40 AM

108 RETWEETS **36** FAVORITES

Taking a closer look at the BLM Movement's "agents of change"

Jay-Z's and Beyoncé's lyrical and financial support for the radical and militant BLM movement and its supporters is extremely troubling on many levels. First, because they are extremely influential nationally and internationally, they are agents of change. Many uninformed teens and young adults admire and pay attention to whatever they say and do. The power couple's public support of the movement empowers and enables it and advances its radical agenda.

Second, the Carters have vast resources to support the BLM movement financially. This support can easily be exploited by leaders of the movement and their radical and militant support groups and members as a means to spread anti-law enforcement, anti-criminal justice, anti-government, pro-black-nationalism, and Marxist propaganda.

Third, the music mogul and his talented superstar wife can use their power and influence in the music industry as recruiting tools to bring more musicians into the movement's fold to increase BLM membership and widen its power base to forward its plans for radical and systemic socialist and/or Marxist change. No matter how you look at Jay-Z's and Beyoncé's support of the militant BLM movement, one thing is obvious: their actions widen the polarizing racial and societal gaps between the white and black communities in America.

Beyoncé usurps 2015 Super Bowl half-time show with anti-police black power statement.

An excellent example of how the Carters use their significant celebrity to forward the false narratives and black nationalist, Black Power message of the Black Lives Matter movement is Beyoncé's recent half-time show during the 2015 season Super Bowl game at the Levi Stadium in Santa Clara, CA.

During the half-time extravaganza, Beyoncé, dressed in a black leather military style uniform and accompanied by ten similarly dressed back-up dancers wearing large afros and sporting black berets resembling the radical, violent black separatist Black Panther Party of the 1960s–1970s, sang and danced to her newest politically charged, anti-police record and video "Formation." Staged in New Orleans, Beyoncé's record video, which has been touted as the "Black Power anthem" for the black community, begins with the singer sitting atop a police car which is immersed in the flood waters of New Orleans. The video single assails law enforcement for police brutality and police responses to 2005's Hurricane Katrina in that city. In her Super Bowl show, Beyoncé also stood atop a police car, which then the sunk beneath the stage - an obvious statement of black power vanquishing law enforcement. One backdrop in the video depicts a wall in which the Black Lives Matter slogan "Stop Shooting Us" is inscribed.

During her presentation, Beyoncé and her black beret adorned dancers raised their fists in the popular "black power" salute first demonstrated by controversial U.S. Olympic Team sprinters John Carlos and Tommie Smith during the 1968 Olympic Games in Mexico City. Beyoncé's dancers then formed an "X," in obvious homage to the controversial radical black separatist Malcolm X.

For the reader who is not aware of who and what the Black Panther Party was, it is important to know that they were a violent, militant black separatist group who murdered police officers and ultimately exploited Oakland's black community. During that period, Black Panther leaders Huey Newton and Eldridge Cleaver embezzled hundreds of thousands of dollars from the Oakland Unified School District's school breakfast fund. Following their indictment, Huey Newton was arrested and imprisoned in California, but Cleaver fled to exile in Cuba, Algeria and France, before making a deal with the feds to return to the U.S. in 1975. It is interesting to note that Cleaver later found God in prison and became a "born-again Christian," joined the Republican Party and voted for Ronald Reagan twice before running twice unsuccessfully for Congress in Southern California as a Republican. Apparently, Beyoncé is not the black history scholar she thinks she is. This is an embarrassment when such an influential member of the black community knows so little about black history.

Beyoncé's very public put-down of law enforcement at a sports venue watched by one billion fans internationally was decried by law enforcement and many supportive of police, such as former New York City Mayor Rudy Giuliani. After watching Beyoncé' and company's act, the mayor commented, "This is football, not Hollywood. I thought it was really outrageous that she used it as a platform to attack police officers, who are the people who protect her and protect us, and keep us alive."[28]

So far, a number of reporters and media commentators, including Fox News' Bill O'Reilly, have reached out to Jay-Z and Beyoncé with interview requests so they can explain the reasons for their quiet, under-the-radar financial support for the BLM movement. However, to date, the couple has elected not to respond. That is also quite troubling.

Jay-Z's and Beyoncé's Human Rights Hypocrisy

While Jay Z and Beyoncé have provided money to the BLM movement to forward their efforts as a "human rights" organization of sorts, at the same time, they were paid $2 million to perform for the son and family of one of the world's most infamous human rights violators – former Libyan dictator Colonel Muammar Gaddafi.

You might recall that it was Gaddafi who accepted responsibility for the terrorist bombing of Pan Am flight 103, on route to New York, by Libyan agent Abdel Basset Ali al-Megrah in Scotland in 1988, killing nearly 300 passengers. Col. Gaddafi greeted the terrorist back into Libya as a hero following his release from prison. Since that time, Libya has paid millions of dollars in reparations to the victims' families.

---

[28] http://www.nydailynews.com/entertainment/beyonce-halftime-show-draws-ire-praise-article-1.2524039

It is well documented that on January 1, 2010, Beyoncé, clad in a skin tight outfit, performed a one-hour set of five songs at the exclusive Nikki Beach Club on the Caribbean island of St. Bart's. The audience included her husband Jay Z, R&B star Usher, hip-hop impresario Russell Simmons, veteran rocker Jon Bon Jovi, singer-actress Lindsay Lohan and Black Entertainment Television owner Bob Johnson. Beyoncé's bill was paid by the murdered dictator's son, Mutassim.

It is both hypocritical and troubling that billionaires Jay-Z and his wife Beyoncé donate money to the BLM movement to further their idea of "civil and human rights" for blacks, while at the same time – and out of the country – freely conducting a lucrative business deal with and entertaining criminal family members of one of the most notorious killers and abusers of human rights in the world, Col. Muammar Gaddafi.

Private funding sources

The Black Lives Matter movement is the same as every other for-profit or non-profit organization with respect to the need for continued funding. The remaining monies that flow into the coffers of the BLM movement come from private donations. The movement depends heavily upon the generosity of its members and supporters.

St. Louis County public records document that on September 16, 2015, BLM movement supporter and St. Louis black talk show host Kenny Murdock, along with BLM movement treasurer James Hill, filed a Statement of Organization for "Black Lives Matter, LLC," requesting status as a Political Action Committee. The group mailed their PAC application to the Federal Election Commission in Washington D.C. on that same day.

Articles in *POLICE* Magazine and the Washington *Post* report that the group has stated its intention to raise funds from the public to make $5,000 donations to various federal candidates who share the group's policy priorities and who accept the donations under an expressed condition to promote the BLM movement's goals and objectives. However, this does not reconcile with other activist groups and organizations under the umbrella of the BLM movement who have repeatedly stated that they do not endorse any candidates or seek the endorsement of any political party.

My research has not been able to establish whether or not the BLM movement as an organization is a 501(c)(3) IRS tax-exempt group. There is a distinct possibility that it is not. If this is the case, then who if anyone in the federal government is monitoring where all of this possible tax-free money is going, how it is being spent, and what taxes the group should be paying the U.S. government?

So what happens if you follow the money? It's almost like a movie plot, but it's true: there *is* a broader conspiracy, an international conspiracy, and the supposed shooting of young blacks is just one more log to throw on the fire. It doesn't matter what the truth is, as long as the movement can get people riled up, tap into long-standing racial anger, and use their false narratives as one more excuse to attack American society and the law enforcement officers that protect it.

References

http://www.opensecrets.org/news/2010/09/opensecrets-battle-koch-brothers/

http://www.discoverthenetworks.org/funderProfile.asp?fndid=5184

http://www.theblaze.com/stories/2012/06/04/special-report-george-soros-godfather-of-the-left/

http://www.discoverthenetworks.org/viewSubCategory.asp?id=589

http://www.washingtontimes.com/news/2015/jan/14/george-soros-funds-ferguson-protests-hopes-to-spur/?page=all

http://www.vibe.com/2015/05/jay-z-Beyoncè-money-protesters-baltimore-ferguson/

http://www.theguardian.com/lifeandstyle/lostinshowbiz/2010/jan/08/Beyoncè-colonel-gaddafi-son

http://www.mediaite.com/online/confirmed-Beyoncè-sings-for-gaddafis-son-on-new-years/

http://www.telegraph.co.uk/news/worldnews/northamerica/usa/8371731/Divas-and-despots-the-stars-who-sing-for-dictators.html

http://www.mediaite.com/online/Beyoncè-new-years-eve-performing-for-gaddafi-family/

http://www.policemag.com/channel/patrol/news/2015/10/27/Black-lives-matter-forms-political-action-committee.aspx

Article, "Black Lives Matter launches a political action committee. But it's not an easy fit," Washington *Post*, Reporter Janell Ross, 10-27-15

http://www.businessinsider.com/beyonce-super-bowl-formation-song-anti-police-2016-2

https://en.wikipedia.org/wiki/Eldridge_Cleaver

http://www.nydailynews.com/entertainment/beyonce-halftime-show-draws-ire-praise-article-1.2524039

http://www.dailymail.co.uk/news/article-3445116/Queen-cynicism-No-stunt-s-shameless-Beyonce-accused-trying-look-white-week-posed-heroine-black-power.html

http://www.nj.com/politics/index.ssf/2016/02/state_troopers_union_blasts_beyonces_halftime_show.html

http://www.nydailynews.com/entertainment/beyonce-halftime-show-draws-ire-praise-article-1.2524039

http://www.msnbc.com/msnbc/beyonce-delivers-politically-charged-super-bowl-halftime-performance

Chapter 7

Black "Lies" Matter – A Movement Founded Upon Falsehoods

On September 2, 2015, I had the pleasure of appearing on Fox News's Megyn Kelly's "Black Lives Matter" (BLM) movement special at the Fox News studios in Manhattan. As someone who has investigated hundreds of high-profile, officer-involved shootings and in-custody deaths, I found the program both fascinating and extremely frustrating.

Gathered together in a "grandstand of guests" format were members of the law enforcement, legal and religious clergy, along with members of the radical BLM movement. I would like to share my experience as a law enforcement and forensic expert, because what I observed that night motivated me to discuss what I believe is an important and core problem with the message of the BLM movement – they tell lies and attempt to promote deliberately false narratives.

Most BLM movement supporters are true believers who won't consider contrary evidence, let alone scientific evidence. In fact, I don't think I'm going out on a limb in claiming that their members spew deliberate lies regarding law enforcement's encounters and uses of force upon members of the black community.

A foundation of falsehoods

What I witnessed that night on Megyn Kelly's special was disconcerting and disquieting, but not unexpected. While my professional colleagues from the law enforcement, legal and religious communities were knowledgeable and articulate in voicing their views regarding the BLM movement, I found the activist members of the movement who voiced their opinions to be uninformed, misinformed and in one case deliberately disingenuous in discussing police encounters with and uses of force, including deadly force, upon black suspects.

It is apparent that the Black Lives Matter movement is founded upon mostly groundless issues, misinformation, and outright falsehoods regarding specific police and civilian-related force encounters with black suspects and persons of interest. Let me now separate the scientific facts from the fantasies on which this movement is based.

In previous chapters, I have provided the non-speculative, objective facts, forensic evidence, and police practices surrounding the fatal encounters between Trayvon Martin and private citizen George Zimmerman and between Michael Brown and Ferguson, MO police officer Darren Wilson.

Both of these incidents formed the foundation for the Black Lives Matter movement, according to its founders Alicia Garza, Patrisse Cullors, Opal Tometi and the Los Angeles BLM Chapter leader professor Melina Abdullah. These incidents and the deaths of felony assailant suspects Martin and Brown are frequently alleged as examples of "extrajudicial murders" of young black men by police and non-black citizens. However, there are other examples of alleged unlawful detentions and arrests and racially motivated acts of "police violence" upon blacks that often surface when BLM leaders and their supporters are marching in protest or are interviewed by the mainstream media. Here are just a couple of examples.

The Sergeant Crowley vs. Professor Gates "unlawful detention" incident

The assertion is that Cambridge police officers, including uniformed Patrol Sergeant James Crowley, racially profiled and unlawfully detained and arrested Harvard Professor Henry Louis Gates, Jr. A review of this incident has proven the allegation to be utterly false.

On July 16, 2009, Cambridge police were dispatched to a residence on Ware Street after receiving a call from neighbor Lucia Whalen, who reported that two unknown black male adults with back packs were on the front porch of a residence and that one of the subjects was attempting to enter the front door by bodily force. Sergeant Crowley was the first officer to arrive on-scene. He spoke with Ms. Whalen and confirmed her observations.

When Sergeant Crowley walked up to the porch of the residence, he observed and encountered Gates, whom he found in the foyer of the home. When the sergeant identified himself, explained the reason for their presence, and asked Gates to step outside to speak with him, the professor replied, "No I will not."

When Sergeant Crowley again explained that he was responding to a possible break-in, Gates replied, "Why, because I'm a black man in America?" When Sergeant Crowley asked Gates if there was anyone else in the home, the professor replied that this was none of the officer's business and accused him of being a "racist."

When Sergeant Crowley directed Gates to produce some identification to verify that he was in fact the resident, Gates ignored him and began to make a phone call. The sergeant overheard Gates telling someone on the other end of the line that he was "dealing with a racist police officer in his home." According to Sergeant Crowley, Gates then told him, "You don't know who you are messing with." Gates then demanded that the uniformed Sergeant Crowley produce his identification.

Now just for a moment, place yourself in the shoes of Sergeant Crowley. You have a neighbor reporting a burglary-in-progress. You arrive and contact the witness, who verifies what she told the police 911 complaint taker. You go to the residence in question alone to investigate a possible felony-in-progress. There you find a black man matching the witness's description in fact inside the home.

As a police officer, you are in full uniform when you contact this suspicious subject. You identify yourself, explain why you are there to this man, whom you don't know and haven't searched for weapons. The man immediately pulls the race card, rather than complying with your respectful and reasonable officer safety requests to tell you if there is anyone else inside the home and to simply step outside to talk with you.

Next, when asked to produce his identification to verify he is in fact the resident, this man not only initially refuses to produce it, but accuses you of racially profiling him. To make matters worse for himself, he demands that you produce your identification instead!

I think you might agree that this is not the best way a well-educated man begins a conversation with a police officer engaged in the lawful investigation of a possible burglary-in-progress, when he is the person of interest and the officer is trying to protect his home from suspected burglars.

Once additional officers, including Harvard University Police officers, arrived on scene, the good Professor Gates reluctantly produced his Harvard University faculty card, instead of a valid driver's license or Massachusetts ID card. Given Gates' previous behavior with Sergeant Crowley, I am inclined to believe that this was Gates' intended and snide "I'm smarter than you. Look how important I am" slight to the officers.

Based upon this information Gates gave them, the Harvard PD officers were able to verify Gates' identity and home address. Sergeant Crowley then apologized to Gates for the inconvenience, and he and the assisting officers left the premises. This should have been the end of this encounter, but it wasn't - not because of anything the officers did, but because the incensed and overly self-important Professor Gates just wouldn't let it go.

As the officers walked away, Gates came out onto his front porch and began to loudly rant and rave about Sergeant Crowley's racial bias, calling him a racist police officer and repeatedly making veiled threats that he and the police had not heard the last of him. Sergeant Crowley took this opportunity to warn Gates that he was now creating a disturbance and advised the agitated professor to calm down or face arrest. When Gates continued his loud verbal tirade, Sergeant Crowley had apparently had enough of the professor's belligerent attitude and arrested him for disorderly conduct. It was just that simple and, in my opinion, a well-deserved and lawful arrest.

Unfortunately, and most probably because Professor Gates had some standing within the Harvard academic community, the prosecutor dropped the charges against Gates. However, the condescending professor was right: Sergeant Crowley and the Cambridge PD had not heard the last from him. Gates had a connection to President Barack Obama, who was apparently on his speed dial.

You may recall that it was President Obama who publically chastised the Cambridge police and Sergeant Crowley on the national news, saying that "the police acted stupidly" for unnecessarily arresting the university professor. It is amazing that the POTUS, who touts himself as a former professor of Constitutional law, knows so little about the laws of arrest and search and seizure and the elements that constitute even basic criminal violations. However, racial bias has been a consistent theme of this President.

In view of the information that the officers had received from a reporting neighbor that he did not recognize a black man who was obviously attempting to break into a residence, Sergeant Crowley and his officers had more than reasonable suspicion to stop/detain Gates. Sergeant Crowley informed Gates why police were at the residence and that he needed to produce some evidence of residency. However, the professor's abnormal, belligerent, and uncooperative demeanor increased rather than decreased the officer's suspicions that Gates might not be the resident.

It was Professor Gates' uncooperative, condescending, "racism," chip-on-his-shoulder attitude and his verbally resistant "I don't have to give you my ID" that prolonged his detention - and nothing else. Later, after police had cleared the scene, it was Professor Gates and not the police who became the provocateur. When Sergeant Crowley warned Gates to calm down or face arrest, the Harvard professor remained verbally non-compliant, loud, disorderly, and in fact threatening.

In the end, Professor Gates' citizen complaint was dropped. The actions of Sergeant Crowley and the other officers were determined to have been appropriate and justified police actions. No civil rights tort was ever filed by the pedantic professor. In fact, it was Professor Gates who inappropriately racially profiled Sergeant Crowley. You see, racism wears many colors. End of story - and of this false narrative about police racially profiling a black man.

The Freddie Gray vs. Baltimore PD Officers in-custody death incident

On April 12th, 2015, police officers working in a high-crime, drug sales area of Baltimore observed 25-year-old recidivist criminal Freddie Gray involved in the possible hand-to-hand sales of drugs. As police approached, Gray fled on foot and was pursued by the officers who captured him. When the officers searched Gray, they found him in possession of a spring-assisted knife which they believed to be illegal. Gray was arrested, handcuffed, and placed into the rear of a transportation van but was not secured in a seat belt.

During transportation to the Western District police station, Gray became agitated and subsequently suffered a serious medical emergency. He was comatose and hospitalized for a serious spinal cord injury and later died on April 19th.

After only a twenty-four-hour investigation by state investigators, six Baltimore officers involved in Freddie Gray's arrest and transportation were charged with several crimes, including second-degree murder in connection with Gray's death.

A leaked Medical Examiner's report of Freddie Gray's autopsy and toxicology reports showed that Gray suffered a devastating spinal cord injury after his head slammed backwards into a wall in the back of the police van. The Medical Examiner who authored the report found no evidence that Gray's spinal injury was caused by any use of police force during his arrest. The forensic medical evidence indicates that Gray broke his neck and that the wound to his head matched an extended metal bolt in the back of the van. The autopsy found no other evidence of trauma that would be consistent with force-related injuries on Gray's body. No police were riding in the back of the van with Gray during his transportation.

Well-known forensic pathologist Dr. Cyril Wecht has opined that Gray's manner of death was consistent with a "rough ride" in the police transportation van. However, my colleague, the eminent forensic pathologist Dr. Vincent DiMaio, who has worked hundreds of high-profile death cases, has suggested that Gray's manner of death should actually be more accurately classified as "accidental or undetermined." As a Certified Medical Investigator myself, I tend to agree with Dr. DiMaio' s opinion at this point.

Another prisoner in the van, identified as Donta Allen, initially told Baltimore investigators and a Washington *Post* reporter that Gray had been agitated, screaming and banging around in the van during transportation. Allen told police and the media that he thought that Gray was "intentionally trying to hurt himself." He has later recanted this statement. A search warrant application describes Gray during transportation as "irate" and that he "continued to be combative in the police wagon."

Freddie Gray's toxicology report showed that he was under the influence of significant levels of cannabinoids and opium at the time he was hospitalized. This finding would be forensically consistent with the possibility of Gray swallowing the drugs he was attempting to sell while fleeing from police in order to destroy evidence. The presence of drugs in Gray's system would also support his past criminal history as a drug dealer. In the past eight years, Gray had been arrested on no less than fourteen occasions for felony possession of controlled substances and possession with intent to distribute. Again, Freddie Gray was only 25 at the time of his death.

The narrative presented by activists, including members of the BLM movement, is that the Baltimore police officers involved in this incident murdered Freddie Gray. There are no forensic evidence or witness statements to date that support this assertion. The autopsy report detailing Gray's traumatic injuries and drug influence - and prisoner

Allen's initial statements to police and the media are far more favorable to the defendant officers than to the prosecution's theory of criminality. Therefore, the BLM movement's assertion that Baltimore police "murdered" Freddie Gray is unsubstantiated at this time

As of this writing, Baltimore State's Attorney Marilyn J. Mosby's chief case against the six Baltimore officers has fallen embarrassingly flat on its face. The state's first case against Police Officer William Porter resulted in a hung jury and a mistrial. Police Officer Edward Nero and police van driver Officer Goodson, Jr., who the state believed they had the strongest case against, have both been acquitted of all charges by black Circuit Judge Barry Williams. The Hon. Judge Williams has publically chastised Ms. Mosby for the manner in which she has presented her cases in court. At this point, it is doubtful that the state will proceed with their prosecutions against the remaining officers Lt. Brian Rice, Sgt. Alicia White and Officer Garrett Miller.

Freddie Gray is no one's hero or role model. In reality, he was a recidivist drug dealing criminal who sold the same poison on the streets that is effectively killing members of Baltimore's black community. Some members of the black community who support Freddie Gray have memorialized him with a painted public mural. While the death of any young man is a tragedy, in my opinion, Freddie Gray is certainly no one who should be memorialized with a public mural. Rather, the people who should be memorialized are the victims of drug-related crime. It's amazing that members of the BLM movement, political activists, and some of the media just don't get this.

Do police officers really kill a disproportionate number of black men?

Perhaps the most damaging, utterly ridiculous and false narrative advanced by the Black Lives Matter movement is that nationally, police officers kill a disproportionate number of black males during encounters.

After hearing it exclaimed time and again by BLM activists, I have determined that they say this as a deliberate scare tactic, hoping that no one will ever do the research and engage them. An excellent example of this tactic is what I heard one activist say on the Megyn Kelly show that I was on.

One BLM member told the audience, "One black man is murdered by police every twenty-eight hours." Really?! Here's the truth and I encourage you to review the research I have listed.

In researching the most recent data from the FBI on homicides nationwide from January, 2009 to the end of 2012, I found that of the 56,250 homicides reported during that period, 1,491 were the result of police uses of force. This equates to an average of roughly 372 persons a year dying as a result of police force intervention.

Of the 1,491 persons who died as a result of police uses of force, 61.4% were white males. Only 32.2% were black males, and 3.2% were males from other races. Females dying as a result of a police use of force comprised the final 3.2% of deaths.

By comparison, of the 56,259 homicides reviewed from 2009–2012, 19,000, or nearly 39%, involved the killing of black males. Of these, only 2.5% involved the death of a black male as a result of a police use of force. In contrast to police officers, private citizen killings of black males in self-defense/justifiable homicides, at 3.4%, were higher than black male deaths attributed to police.

What stands out as a significant and shocking statistic is that 17,719 criminal homicides (murders) of black males, or 93.3% from 2009–2012, were at the hands of other criminals who were predominately other black males (89.6%). This is what is referred to as "black-on-black crime."

In sharp contrast to the false narrative that police officers have some racial motivation to kill black men, from 2009–2012, nearly 41% of murdered police officers were killed by black males; compare this to the 32% black male homicide rate mentioned above. This is significant, given the fact that blacks as a whole comprise only 13% of the U.S. population of over 316,000,000, and there are less than 900,000 peace officers in this country, including many who do not work in a street patrol capacity.

To put this study into perspective, an average of 120 black males, or one out of every 173,871 black males, die yearly as a result of police uses of force, versus 2,369 black males being killed in motor vehicle accidents and 2,532 committing suicide each year.

When all homicides of black male statistics are considered, black males are 35 times more likely to be murdered by another black male; 20 times more prone to die in a motor vehicle accident or by suicide; and 21 times more susceptible to being killed in a self-defense, justifiable homicide than killed by any police use of force.

A few more numbers: an average of 120 black males die each year as a result of a police use of force. University of Toledo Professor Richard Johnson's research has found that the chances that a black man will be killed by police, is less than their chances of being killed by a lightning strike. I also researched this. Research documents that from 1995 – 2002, 374 persons were are struck/killed by lightning in the U.S. This averages out to 0.23 lightening deaths per million persons per year. During that same eight-year period, only nine black males were struck/killed by lightning.[29] In essence, Dr. Johnson is correct. The chance of a black male dying as a result of police force intervention is statistically considerably far less than his chances of being struck by lightning. That's far from the BLM movement's assertion that police kill one black male every twenty-eight hours.

Further, the BLM movement's pseudo research and false assertion that police kill a black man every 28 hours just doesn't reconcile using *their* numbers. There are approximately 1,251 28-hour periods in the four-year period from 2009 – 2012. That is presumably how many black

---

[29] http://www.bls.gov/iif/oshwc/cfoi/jeh5_05_45-50.pdf

males would have been killed by police during this period if the BLM movement claim was true. However, 32.2% of 1,491 deaths is only 480 deaths. So, the "every 28-hours" claim is off by a whopping 250%.

By the way, recent officers injured/killed in the line of duty statistics also show that upwards of 80% of suspects who injure or kill officers are armed with weapons; 70% of those suspects are armed with handguns. So the BLM assertion that police officers are simply killing unarmed black men without cause or for some arbitrary reason is blatantly false.

Summary: Just what is emerging here?

It is every American's civil right to protest against the government. Colonial Americans protested against British oppression, excessive taxation, and unreasonable searches and seizures of their persons and property, even before this nation was formally established. Non-violent protest can be healthy, informative and change-effecting. However, the Black Lives Matter movement is none of those things. It is a violent group that cannot control its members, and that's a scary thought.

Anytime a group marches and openly chants violent and life threatening rhetoric such as screaming, "Pigs in a blanket; fry 'em like bacon" and "What do we want? Dead cops! When do we want them? Now!", as we recently observed in Minnesota and in downtown New York City, we need to be concerned for our safety.

That is how Adolph Hitler with his brown-shirted Nazi party, Mussolini and his Black-shirted Fascists, and Vladimir Lenin and his communists began their movements. If you recall, all of these movements began their ascents into power by spreading false narratives. It is also important to keep in mind that the Black Lives Matter movement is immersed in Marxist revolutionary and Black Nationalist ideology. So the lies they repeatedly shout in the streets and in front of the TV cameras closely resemble the rhetoric of these past revolutionary movements.

To put all of the BLM movement's misrepresentations and lies into context and comparison with the behavior of law enforcement: we have yet to see a police officer walk up behind a black man who was putting gas into his car, shoot him in the back of the head and then pump fifteen more bullets into his lifeless body before walking away unconcerned as black cop killer Shannon Miles did to Harris County, Texas Deputy Darren Goforth on August 28, 2015.

We have yet to see a police officer waltz up to two black men sitting peacefully in a car, shoot them both in the head execution style, and then exclaim on social media that he was out "to put wings on a couple of pigs today" as black cop killer Ismaaiyl Brinsley did to New York PD patrol Officers Wenjian Liu and Rafael Ramos on December 20, 2014. It's just that simple.

I am not concerned about the BLM's response that "only a relative few" of their members are extremists who shout violent rhetoric and commit acts of violence during demonstrations. It's just another false narrative not substantiated by the many video news stories documenting hundreds of Black Lives Matter movement supporters chanting violent, anti-police rhetoric. I am concerned that this entire movement was founded and exists primarily upon a pack of lies. And you should be too.

Who's really to blame for black problems?

The BLM movement is about assigning blame to police, but refusing to accept ownership and responsibility for the endemic problems historically plaguing the urban and rural black communities for decades. The police did not create pregnant tweens; families without fathers; or a 50% high school dropout rate. The police are not responsible for drug sales and addiction. Police and the municipal and federal governments are not responsible for the creation of murderous street gangs preying on their own communities and killing young black adolescents and young adults.

The police are not responsible for glorifying gangsta rappers who refer to black women as "bitches" and "ho's." Police officers are not responsible for encouraging impressionable young black men to prioritize drug money over family and faith. Law enforcement is not responsible for an ever soaring black-on-black inner city homicide rate. The police don't create these problems; they *respond* to them. That's their mission and their responsibility.

If the members of the BLM movement and some of the enabling liberal politicians and media really want to get to the root causes of the polarization between themselves, a relative minority of the black community, and law enforcement, I suggest that they take a deep breath and a hard look into the mirror to see how we got where we are today.

It is also important for the reader to understand that the vast majority of blacks and black communities are not supporters of the Black Lives Matter movement or their extremist radical counterparts who spew violent rhetoric.

I heard a number of the good people on the dais with me during Megyn Kelly's Black Lives Matter special who spoke of the need for unification, mutual cooperation, and the re-prioritization of family and faith. Law enforcement can work with that. However, they cannot work with those who believe that police are government terrorists with a mission to systematically murder young black men without provocation in "extrajudicial killings." And they will not work with those who openly advocate for the killing of police officers. Who would?

However, the good people of the black community have to speak up to assertively renounce the Black Lives Matter movement and its violent rhetoric and disruptive actions. If they do not do this, then this nation will see levels of violence like never before. It's just that simple. The question is: do the involved parties have the heroic courage and commitment needed to fix it?

References

http://www.thesmokinggun.com/documents/crime/henry-louis-gates-jr-police-report

http://www.thesmokinggun.com/file/henry-louis-gates-jr-police-report

http://www.foxnews.com/politics/2010/06/30/review-harvard-professor-arrest-finds-incident-avoidable/

http://www.justice.gov/opa/pr/justice-department-announces-findings-two-civil-rights-investigations-ferguson-missouri

http://www.justice.gov/sites/default/files/opa/press-releases/attachments/2015/03/04/doj_report_on_shooting_of_michael_brown_1.pdf

http://www.nationalreview.com/article/420274/freddy-gray-autopsy-report-deals-blow-murder-charges-andrew-c-mccarthy

http://dailycaller.com/2015/05/06/claim-task-force-investigating-freddie-gray-death-came-to-different-conclusion-than-states-attorney/

http://twitchy.com/2015/06/23/newspaper-leaks-freddie-gray-autopsy-death-ruled-an-accident-enabled-by-police-acts-of-omission/

http://dailycaller.com/2015/06/24/law-professor-freddie-gray-autopsy-is-very-very-helpful-to-the-defense/2/

http://nation.foxnews.com/2015/04/30/freddie-gray-arrest-record-criminal-history-rap-sheet

http://nypost.com/2015/04/30/freddie-gray-killed-by-head-slamming-into-bolt-in-police-van-report/

http://www.washingtonpost.com/local/crime/prisoner-in-van-said-freddie-gray-was-banging-against-the-walls-during-ride/2015/04/29/56d7da10-eec6-11e4-8666-a1d756d0218e_story.html

http://www.cnn.com/2015/05/01/us/freddie-gray-van-second-man/

http://www.msnbc.com/msnbc/police-freddie-gray-arrested-switchblade

https://www.washingtonpost.com/politics/michael-brown-shooting-protesters-police-clash-overnight-in-ferguson-mo/2014/08/12/733985e6-2220-11e4-8593-da634b334390_story.html

http://www.nbcnews.com/watch/nbc-news/obama-comments-on-michael-brown-shooting-334518339771

http://www.cnn.com/2009/US/07/22/harvard.gates.interview

http://www.bls.gov/iif/oshwc/cfoi/jeh5_05_45-50.pdf

Chapter 8

#Every28hours – The disproportionate police killing of black men: the birth (and continued life) of a lie

While I was appearing as a guest expert on Fox News's "Black Lives Matter" special with host Megyn Kelly, two of the Black Lives Matter (BLM) activists who were discussing the issue of excessive force by police upon black suspects casually tossed out the comment that "Every 28 hours, an unarmed black man is killed by police." I was keenly aware that the comment was false. However, I was amazed that I was the only law enforcement professional present who had actually researched the subject to know this was so.

Having researched and recently written about both the Black Lives Matter movement and the actual statistics of black suspects dying during police encounters nationwide, I have been disappointed by the mainstream media's and the public's ignorance that the "Every 28 hours…" comment is simply one of several false narratives consistently presented as a "fact" whenever members of the BLM movement, other anti-police activist groups, or their liberal mouthpieces appear at protest marches or on TV. To my knowledge, no one in the media has challenged this comment, thus perpetuating this blatant falsehood. Here is the documented history of this comment.

Background: how it all started

After the now infamous officer-involved shooting death of strong-arm robbery suspect and police assailant Michael Brown by Officer Darren Wilson in Ferguson, MO, there was a CNN debate on August 20, 2014, between black conservative talk show host Larry Elder and liberal New York black professor Marc Lamont Hill. Professor Hill commented that "Every 28 hours an unarmed black person is killed by police."

Challenged by a reporter from *Fact Check* on August 27, 2014, Professor Hill later recanted, conceding that the accusation was "incorrect." However, the damage had already been done. The erroneous factoid went viral over the Internet and unfortunately remains with us today. So where did Professor Hill and others pick up the "Every 28 hours…" comment?

The lie actually comes from a liberal writer identified as Arlene Eisen, who produced a report in April, 2013, entitled "Operation Ghetto Storm," which was then published by the militant Malcolm X Grassroots Movement. Ms. Eisen, who has no knowledge or skills as a scientific forensic researcher, conducted her own limited "research" into the deaths of 313 black men, women and children who were killed in 2012.

To obtain the figure of a black person's death "every 28 hours," Ms. Eisen simply divided the number of hours in a year (8,760) by her number of black deaths (313). Well, there you go - an instant and provocative statistic that seems to resonate with black and liberal anti-police activists like members of the BLM movement. The only problem is that Ms. Eisen is a self-appointed pseudo-researcher whose "research" and report were extremely biased and scientifically flawed.

Debunking the pseudo-research

After Ms. Eisen finished her report, she quickly put it out on the Internet, complete with the provocative hashtag, #Every28hours. Her report, based upon specious research, has generated tremendous interest within the Black Lives Matter movement and the liberal mainstream media.

It is important that people and the media who freely toss out statistics from Eisen's now admittedly flawed "Operation Ghetto Storm" report know that Eisen did *not* deal solely with *police-involved* deaths of black men. And it included not only black men, but also *women and teens*.

Even more important: the report's figures included not only police-involved deaths, but deaths as a result of encounters with off-duty police officers working private security jobs, non-sworn civilian private security guards, and private citizens - all of whom claimed to have shot their assailants in circumstances of self-defense, according to police reports and media accounts.

That is a huge and deliberate skewing of the statistical data, which completely misrepresents the numbers of black men and blacks in general dying during police encounters. To make matters worse, Ms. Eisen even included cases of accidental discharges of firearms when there was absolutely no intent of the armed individuals to fire their weapon at anyone.

In an article Ms. Eisen wrote in September, 2013, she attempted to justify her research by stating that the intent of her report was "to prevent future extrajudicial killings of black people by those paid or sanctioned [security guards and private citizen "vigilantes"] by the national security state. It is important to know that these killings are a result of the perpetual war on black people."

Does anyone besides me see a personal, inherent, emotional, and political research bias here? Where exactly is the evidence for a "perpetual war"?

When Fact Checker reporters challenged Ms. Eisen's research methodology, she conceded that including non-police related shootings did not necessarily fit her personal theory that there is a police "war against black people." However, reporter Michelle Ye Hee Lee notes that Eisen continues to insist that her study "does point out that there is systemic problem of law enforcement and 'other extrajudicial killers' using excessive force that is not justifiable by law."

Eisen also concedes that the figures and statistics in her report are not accurate. She concludes,

"I don't think that the burden should be on me to prove that [my statistics are] an accurate list. I'm not saying it's completely accurate. If you want a full count, you should demand it from the Department of Justice."

In summary, it is truly both unfortunate and disappointing that the mainstream media and the general public allow themselves to be spoon-fed by biased and self-serving report authors like Arlene Eisen. The tragedy here is that if Ms. Eisen had followed her own advice and conducted ethical, scientific research of the most accurate and publically available statistics on police-involved death cases from the U.S. Department of Justice, the National Institute of Justice, and the FBI, her now infamous and blatantly false assertion would never have become an anti-police rallying cry for the Black Lives Matter movement and other misinformed anti-police activists.

Hopefully, this chapter will help put the false narrative to rest once and for all.

Are police officers really disproportionally killing black men? Providing truth to another false narrative

Among several prominent false narratives being unethically disseminated by anti-law enforcement activists and an uninformed media is that police officers kill black men at a rate that is disproportionate to other races.

Those who criticize police after officer-involved shootings and in-custody deaths immediately allege racism is the root cause. But is this factually accurate and fair? A recent study by University of Toledo criminal justice professor Dr. Richard Johnson which I mentioned in the previous chapter shows that this is not the case.

You'll recall that according to FBI nationwide homicide data from 2009-12, 1,491 people died as a result of police uses of force. Over 61% of these were white males, 32.2% were black males, and 3.2% were males from other races. The remaining 3.2% were females.

Of all 56,000 homicides in those four years, 19,000, or nearly 39%, involved the killing of black males. As I mentioned before, of these 19,000, *only 2.5%* involved the death of a black male as a result of a police use of force. In contrast to police officers, the percent of black males killed by civilians in self-defense (justifiable homicides), at 3.4%, was *higher* than the percent of black male deaths attributed to police.

Putting police-involved black deaths into forensic perspective: being struck by lightning

To put this vetted research study into perspective, an average of 120 black males, or about one out of every 173,000, die yearly as a result of police uses of force. Compare that to the 2,369 black males being killed in motor vehicle accidents and 2,532 committing suicide each year. In fact, as I noted above, a *black male is 35 times more likely to be murdered by another black male; 20 times more prone to die in a motor vehicle accident or by suicide; and 21 times more susceptible to being killed in a self-defense, justifiable homicide than killed by any police use of force.*

What about the police officers? From 2009–12, 224 police officers were murdered, and nearly 60,000 sustained injuries from assaults by violently assaultive and/or resisting suspects. During the decade from 2004–14, over 57,000 officers have been violently assaulted by suspects.

The anti-law-enforcement sentiment is rapidly growing in America, and several false narratives are being spread by those who, like members of the Black Lives Matter movement and their surrogates, would seek to undermine the efforts of the vast majority of law enforcement officers who face the very risky, difficult, and challenging task of policing urban and rural communities.

Why and when do police use force? What the numbers tell us

What is never mentioned in any discussion of police uses of force in the minority community is a factually consistent theme of *disrespect for legal authority and resistance during detention and/or arrest that results in police use of force.*

With over 900,000 municipal, state and federal officers in the United States generating *tens of millions* of citizen contacts each month, it is important to keep in mind that police use force in only 1%-2% of those contacts. During those contacts where force is used, only an extremely small fraction of that percentage results in an officer-involved shooting or an in-custody death.

In literally *every* one of the nearly three hundred cases of serious uses of force, including officer-involved shootings (OIS) and in-custody deaths (ICD), suspects who were seriously injured; shot and killed; or died in police custody had either violently resisted capture and arrest and/or were engaged in a violent armed felony when police encountered them. These data are consistent with my observations, over a thirty-six-year career, of the death cases I have investigated and analyzed involving police-suspect encounters that result in fatalities.

Perhaps if members of the BLM movement want to seriously delve into the causes of police use of force upon members of the black and minority communities, they should seek real solutions to the anti-authority and police resistance behaviors exhibited by those within their community. When law enforcement officers encounter, under criminal circumstances, aggressive individuals who threaten them and resist detention, capture, control, and arrest, who exactly is responsible for the violence that results?

References

"Examining the Prevalence of Death from Police Use of Force," Johnson, Richard, Ph.D., © 2015, University of Toledo

U.S. Dept. of Justice, FBI Uniform Crime Report Supplemental Homicide Reports and U.S. Center for Disease Control death classifications, Jan. 2009 – Jan. 2012

National Safety Council, *Injury Facts* (2012), www.nsc.org

www.cdc.gov/violenceprevention/suicide/statistics/aag.html

www.usatoday.com/weather/resources/basics/wlighting.htm

http://drronmartinelli.com/2015/06/22/police-officers-disproportionally-killing-Black-men-another-false-narrative/

http://drronmartinelli.com/2015/09/05/Black-lies-matter-the-forensic-facts-behind-the-false-narratives-of-this-violent-anti-police-movement/

https://mxgm.org/operation-ghetto-storm-2012-annual-report-on-the-extrajudicial-killing-of-313-Black-people/

"An unarmed Black person is shot 'every 28 hours' says Marc Lamont Hill," Sanders, Katie, © 08-26-14, After the Fact

"The viral claim that a Black person is killed by police 'every 28 hours'," Ye Hee Lee, Michelle, © 12-24-14, FactChecker.com

"1 Black Man is Killed Every 28 Hours by Police or Vigilantes: America is Perpetually at War with its Own People," Hudson, Adam, © 05-28-13, Alternet.org

Chapter 9

#Every 96 Minutes – The Forensic Facts Behind the Deaths of Black Men

The Inconvenient Truth of 'Black-On-Black' Homicide

After conducting socio-criminal research on police-involved death cases and black homicides nationally, I found significant differences between what is being falsely presented by anti-police activists and an uninformed media and the actual known forensic facts of the circumstances of the deaths of black men.

After researching and debunking the false narrative that police kill unarmed black men "every 28 hours," I decided to dig deeper to discover what the factual statistics were for black men being murdered in *non-police* related violent crimes. My findings are both startling and scary for the black community. The statistics also provide you with better context when comparing incidents of police-involved deaths of blacks to black-on-black homicides.

According to the U.S. Census Bureau, there are currently about 21.5 million black males in the U.S. – only about 6% of the total population.

Do black lives really matter to blacks?

Well, that all depends upon *whom* you ask. If you ask the families of the black men, women, and small children victims killed by other black men, it matters. However, if you ask black activists and BLM movement protesters and their supporters if *other* Black Lives Matter, you quickly find that they are adept at practicing deflection and redirection away from the inconvenient truth that *blacks murder other blacks at an alarming and disproportionate rate*. In other words, they just don't seem to care.

Recent statistics for homicides in the City of Chicago

To provide some recent context regarding the problem of black- on-black homicides, from January 1 - March 8, 2016 in the City of Chicago, there were a total of 558 shootings, resulting in 463 persons being wounded and 95 persons being killed. Eighty-four percent (84.4%) of Chicago homicides were as a result of gun violence. Of these, an overwhelming majority of 71% were black homicides, with Hispanics accounting for 24%, and whites and other races comprising the remaining 4.7% of those deaths. A "2016 Shot Time Clock" developed by independent researchers calculated that in the City of Chicago, a person is shot every 2:56 minutes and one is murdered every 14:42 hours.[30] That is truly amazing. In sharp contrast, Chicago police had killed only *one* person and wounded none by the same date in 2016. So exactly *who* are the violent people here?

Chicago's 2016-gun violence rate is certainly far from being an aberration. Statistics show that in 2015, the city had 2,939 shooting victims and 460 homicides. There were 416 homicides in 2014 and 420 murders in 2013. The city's worst homicide rate was in 2012, when 506 of its citizens were murdered. Again, the vast majority of these homicides involved black assailants and victims.[31]

Members of the BLM movement and other radical, militant groups and their supporters will march on city halls; they will close off entire freeways; and they will loot and burn down mostly black-owned and black-employing businesses in protest of a police shooting of a resistant criminal suspect. However, the execution-style murder of a nine-year-old-son of a black gang member by another gang member or nine-year-old Tyshawn Lee, who was lured into an alley and executed by 22-year-old black parolee Dwight Boone-Doty, only three months after being released from prison for unlawful possession and use of a firearm by a

---

[30] 2016 Chicago Murder Crime Statistics, www.heyjackass.com

[31] 2012 – 2015 Chicago Murder Crime Statistics, www.chicagotribune.com

felon and other narcotics convictions does not seem to resonate with them.

The leaders and supporters of the BLM movement appear to be completely disengaged from the outrage of the premeditated murders of small children and other innocents. In fact, you can't find three of them to form a protest line to voice their dissent. Where does this mentality come from? I can't tell you, but I do know that it is very troubling: blacks who say they care about black well-being, yet denying and refusing to candidly discuss the systematic slaughter of their own people – *by their own people*.

The Department of Justice/FBI Uniform Crime Reports indicate that between 2009 and 2012, there about 40,300 homicides of males. Of these, 22,020 of the victims were black. Therefore, during those four years, black males made up approximately 52.2% of all male and female homicide victims in the United States.

In conducting similar socio-criminal research, University of Toledo criminologist Professor Richard Johnson, Ph.D., found that 90% of black male homicides are committed by *another black male*.

Despite recent controversy created by black activists and biased pseudo-researchers who claim that a disproportionate number of black males die in police encounters each year, the mainstream media rarely if ever verify the fabricated statistics fed to them. In fact, as noted above, the U.S. Department of Justice and FBI's Uniform Crime Reports (UCR) document that only 32.2% of the 1,491 total officer-involved deaths of citizens between the years 2009 –2012 were black males.

More white males die during encounters with police. In fact, as I have previously researched and written, private *citizens* actually kill *more* black males (usually in self-defense) than police do.

Research methodology and findings

How were the statistical data in this book collected and scientifically calculated?

U.S. DOJ/FBI and UCR reports and NIBRS data was collected on homicide rates of black males nationwide. Next, the number of days each year for the years 2009–2012, along with the total hours for that four-year period, was calculated.

Next, Professor Johnson's black homicide statistics were integrated into our formula in order to obtain a more accurate figure for the rate of black-on-black homicides per twenty-four-hour period. It is important to note that our statistics also include previously unreported *multiple homicides* per incident, when those circumstances were documented to have occurred.

Here is what I have determined. There were a total of 1,461 days during the four-year period 2009–2012. When you divide by the total black homicide rate of 22,020 victims by 1,461 days, you find that 15 black males are killed every 24 hours. When the figure of 15 black male victims is then divided by 24 hours, the result is 0.625 victims per hour; or roughly one black male homicide every *96 minutes*.

A disturbing context of crime

There is no other racial group in the United States that has this internal homicide rate. To recap the numbers I presented above, blacks comprise about 13% of the entire U.S. population. Of that, 48% are black males – about 6.6% of the total U.S. Of this group, only 61% of black males are under 65 years of age.[32] However, in the four years from 2009–2012, black males – only 6% of the nation's population -

---

[32] www.BlackDemographics.com

accounted for approximately 52.2% of *all* male and female homicide victims in the United States.

Within the black community, a relatively small group of black men commits over 90% of all homicides of black males. In 2012, white males comprised 38% of the U.S. population and were responsible for 4,582 murders. In contrast, that same year, black males committed 5,531 homicides, in which approximately 90% of the victims were black males. In other words, *a group one-fifth the size of their white counterparts murdered 1,000 more victims. This is significant.*

If one compares these staggering black homicide statistics with officer-involved fatal shootings of black males, one finds that *at the current rate, it would take police officers about forty years to kill as many black men as were murdered by other black men in 2012 alone!*

Black murder and combat death

To provide you with more context, I offer a comparison of the black-on-black homicide rate during only a four-year period (2009–2012), to that of U.S. military combat causalities during several of our most notable wars and conflicts. Black-on-black homicides for the years 2009–2012 (22,020) were:

- 4.57 times or 457% higher than the combined death toll of American soldiers (4,815) during the twelve-year Operation Iraqi Freedom war (2003–2015)
- 6.2 times or 620% higher than the combined death toll of American soldiers (3,506) during the fourteen-year Operation Enduring Freedom/Afghanistan war (2001–2015)
- 2.6 times or 264% higher than the combined total military deaths from both wars (8,321)
- Nearly 38% of all fatal military combat causalities (58,220) from the 20 year Vietnam War (1955–1975)
- 65% of all fatal military combat causalities (33,652) from the Korean War (1950–1953)

41% of all fatal military combat causalities (53,402) from World War I (1917 – 1918)

- 2.7 times or 275% of all fatal military combat causalities from the 8-year American Revolutionary War (1775–1783)

Now this is really something to ponder. Better yet, ask yourself why the co-founders, leaders, supporters of the Black Lives Matter movement and other well-known politicians, vocal "community activists," and the mainstream news media never provide such figures and context, in any conversation, about the alarming black homicide rate in America.

I know why. It is most likely because these statistics are astounding and do not reconcile with their false narratives that police are killing young black males.

Just think of it. Every ninety-six minutes, a black male is murdered in America - and more likely than not by another black male. *What afflicts the black community is not the police committing "extrajudicial homicides" of black males. It is actually black males committing daily acts of black genocide.*

The members of the BLM movement deflect and redirect the conversation by telling Americans and those in the international community, "Don't pay attention to the violent criminal black man behind the curtain. It's really the cops who are murdering our people."

The leaders of the Black Lives Matter movement have learned that the more they spout this false narrative, the more people will believe it. The only problem is – it's a blatant lie. And now you know the one of the significant truths behind the lies that form the foundation of the BLM movement. It is a lie with deadly consequences for black people.

References

"Examining the Prevalence of Death from Police Use of Force," Johnson, Richard, Ph.D., © 2015, University of Toledo

U.S. Dept. of Justice, FBI Uniform Crime Report Supplemental Homicide Reports and U.S. Center for Disease Control death classifications, Jan. 2009 – Jan. 2012.

National Safety Council, Injury Facts (2012), www.nsc.org

www.cdc.gov/violenceprevention/suicide/statistics/aag.html

www.usatoday.com/weather/resources/basics/wlighting.htm

www.heyjackass.com

http://www.chicagotribune.com/news/local/breaking/ct-chicago-police-violence-2015-met1-20160101-story.html

http://drronmartinelli.com/2015/06/22/police-officers-disproportionally-killing-Black-men-another-false-narrative/

http://drronmartinelli.com/2015/09/05/Black-lies-matter-the-forensic-facts-behind-the-false-narratives-of-this-violent-anti-police-movement/

https://mxgm.org/operation-ghetto-storm-2012-annual-report-on-the-extrajudicial-killing-of-313-Black-people/

http://www.BlackDemographics.com

https://en.wikipedia.org/wiki/Vietnam_War_casualties

https://en.wikipedia.org/wiki/United_States_military_casualties of war

"An unarmed Black person is shot 'every 28 hours' says Marc Lamont Hill," Sanders, Katie, © 08-26-14, After the Fact

"The viral claim that a Black person is killed by police 'every 28 hours'," Ye Hee Lee, Michelle, © 12-24-14, FactChecker.com

"1 Black Man is Killed Every 28 Hours by Police or Vigilantes: America is Perpetually at War with its Own People," Hudson, Adam, © 05-28-13, Alternet.org

Chapter 10
Why the news media don't get it

As a national media consultant/expert for major news outlets, I find myself continually shocked at the media's complete lack of understanding of even basic police practices and legal issues, such as laws of arrest and search and seizure. Media pundits and talking heads continually get it wrong when describing or opining on police actions during encounters with resistive, verbally threatening, physically resistant, and/or armed subjects who pose great dangers to police and the general public.

In fact, I have found that some of the national media commentators who are most revered by the public actually know little to nothing about basic police procedures and the use of force, despite the fact that crime and policing news accounts for a quarter of the air time on every local or national news program.

Why don't news reporters and commentators "get" what law enforcement and police officers do? Well, from my standpoint, both behind and in front of the camera, I have learned that the pressures of the 24/7 news cycle are so intense and rapidly evolving that the field journalists, fact-checkers, associate producers, editors, and producers who obtain information, edit it, and then provide the copy to the talking-head commentators we see on television simply don't have time to produce a quality three-minute sound bite that accurately reflects the circumstances or incident fact pattern. Thus the public does not get an objective account of why police officers took the actions they did, actions that ultimately resulted in a serious or deadly use of force.

News "readers," not investigators

Very few national news commentators I have met come from the "Walter Cronkite School of Journalistic Ethics." Most of them are highly-paid "readers" of the news, rather than "investigators" of the objective facts that comprise the news. However, the general public does not know this, so they simply believe whatever commentators say because they "like" them.

In all fairness, very few of America's high-profile national news readers/commentators are physically able to objectively investigate and report the news accurately because they simply lack the time to do so. The 24/7 news cycle provides them with little time to devote to the forensic facts of any case.

Any time they want to spend researching a high-profile, Michael-Brown-shooting-type police story, they must compete with multiple other news program obligations, travel, spending time on their various personal news blogs, news briefings with associate producers, spending time in the make-up room, and final set preparation.

By the way, they also have the demands of their own lives and family time to contend with. However, I do believe that it is the responsibility of on-air news commentators to ensure that the news copy that does reach them is vetted and factually unbiased.

Anti-police bias in the news media

We have all experienced blatant media bias, whether we are actually police officers or just members of the general public. Sometimes while watching a news story about a police action, especially a use of deadly force, I listen to the reporter or news commentator make a stupid, uninformed, or flagrantly biased comment about how the responding officers handled a very difficult and high-risk incident, and I want to throw something at my TV screen.

Anyone who truly believes that members of the Fourth Estate are not biased is simply living in a bubble. Media bias is everywhere in the reporting of both politics and police actions.

Reporters and news commentators have their own personal, political, and/or cultural agendas and apparently have no scruples about airing their non-objective, speculative opinions disguised as "breaking news." I see this all of the time, and I don't believe that it will ever change. This is just a painful reality that the law enforcement community must deal with.

I am a forensic expert who is paid to face intense scrutiny of my work product and opinions in every case I am retained in, from aggressive opposing attorneys to judges. I always consider that every attorney and judge is smarter than I - unless they prove to me otherwise during our encounters in a deposition or in a courtroom. Therefore, allow me to provide some simple advice to law enforcement administrators who face the often skeptical and aggressive news media.

Police administrators, Public Information Officers and detectives need to remember that reporters and commentators control the questions, but you control the *answers*. Always have your facts right and know what to say, when to say it and, most importantly, *how* to say it when addressing the media. Remain on point and never get distracted or emotionally captured when you are making those points before the camera, and, generally speaking, you should do fine.

One example of political and cultural reporting bias I experienced as a media expert occurred when I was asked by a major national news outlet to compile and forensically analyze the circumstances and evidence in the infamous private-citizen shooting of Trayvon Martin by George Zimmerman. I had painstakingly done my research and presented my report and findings to a producer, only to have him respond, after reading the report that they were not going to use any of my information in their news stories. That analysis is found in Chapter 2.

While frustrated with the producer's response, I must admit that I wasn't really surprised, considering that this same news outlet had aired a number of broadcasts that were consistently supportive of Zimmerman's conviction for the crime of "murdering" Trayvon Martin.

Contrary to the news media's opinion that Zimmerman was criminally culpable in Martin's death, I believe that if you consider all of the objective facts and forensic evidence in this case, including the very damaging facts about Martin that were excluded from the jury's consideration, you will see that this case was really a no-brainer and that George Zimmerman was factually innocent in the self-defense homicide of Trayvon Martin.

Ultimately, the controversy that created the opportunity for the Black Lives Matter movement to use this incident as a key building block in the foundation of their organization was precipitated by three things: (1) Trayvon Martin was a black teen, and George Zimmerman was a Hispanic Caucasian, so there were obvious racial overtones; (2) the politics of the anti–"stand your ground" gun control lobby; and (3) overt media bias promoted by hashtag journalists who believed that Zimmerman was guilty all along and were simply not interested in the objective facts and forensic evidence that would exonerate him.

The media keep getting it wrong.

In a number of recent, high-profile, police-involved death cases, the news media have been complicit in getting it wrong.

Examples include the stories about Michael Brown ("Officer shoots/kills unarmed black teen;" Ferguson, MO); Tamir Rice ("Police shoot/kill 12-year-old black boy holding plastic gun"; Cleveland, OH); Officer Michael Brelo ("Brelo and 12 other police officers shoot/kill two innocent people in vehicle"; Cleveland, OH); and Ezell Ford ("Police shoot/kill unarmed black homeless man;" Los Angeles, CA) - these are just a few incidents of bad and/or biased and factually inaccurate reporting that have enabled and empowered black activists such as the BLM movement to build upon their militant anti-police political platform.

These stories, with their incomplete, uninformed, factually incorrect, and in some cases deliberately false narratives, have significantly exacerbated the polarization between the black and law enforcement communities.

In turn, the dissent, activism, and violent militancy displayed by revolutionary and violent activists such as those of the BLM movement,

Occupy, and others in rioting, looting, and burning down predominately black-owned businesses have provided the 24/7 news media with a never-ending cycle of breaking news stories, higher ratings, and increased revenues.

On the other hand…

I have worked with a number of local and major national news media outlets, reporters, and independent journalists who sincerely care about the accurate and unbiased reporting of police and crime news. For instance, I have had the pleasure of working on several occasions with black CNN reporter Stephanie Elam and her crew from the Los Angeles CNN outlet on the Michael Brown shooting and other high-profile shooting cases.

In the Michael Brown case, I was able to explain the importance of the forensic evidence found in Officer Darren Wilson's patrol SUV and its significance to the objective fact pattern in that case.

I was also able to demonstrate on camera the human factors issues of "reactionary gap," action-reaction perception lag time, and the "21-foot rule" before a national audience. Following my appearance, I received hundreds of emails from the law enforcement and forensic communities and the general public in appreciation of this unique perspective on police practices and case analysis.

But the credit should not go to me - I was simply the conduit of information. My job is to investigate, analyze and educate. The real credit goes to Ms. Elam and her crew for having the courage, professional ethics and insight to bring these important issues to the general public so that people were able to understand the case more clearly.

Fox News commentator Bill O'Reilly is one of the great national news media hosts who "gets it" with respect to providing a fair and balanced accounting of the objective facts of high-profile, police-involved death news cases. I have been on O'Reilly's show on a couple of occasions and find him to be an astute, no-nonsense commentator who asks the hard questions. This is the hallmark of a news professional.

From a professional standpoint, I think that Mr. O'Reilly stands head and shoulders above his nationally ranked colleagues because he had a solid background as a hard news reporter before becoming a commentator and host of *The O'Reilly Factor*. His ratings are consistently the highest in the industry because he works the hardest to put out a quality news product. O'Reilly is also smart enough to separate news from his personal opinions, while his competitors simply blend the two together.

Another media commentator who objectively analyzes police crime news is veteran Cleveland radio talk show host Bob Frantz, of the "Bob Frantz Authority" at WHK Radio AM 1420, *The Answer*. I can always depend on Bob Frantz to ask the right questions so that he and his listeners can get to the facts and the bottom line of every news story involving law enforcement.

Summary

America's Fourth Estate news industry has a critical responsibility, as well as an ethical and moral obligation, to gather all of the facts and to report police-involved crime stories fairly and accurately without politics and personal biases. I recall, years ago, a research project commissioned by the American Bar Association. The ABA reported that 90% of the American people learn 90% about what they know about police and policing by watching television and going to the movies.

Television shows and movies generally negatively portray law enforcement either as dark, troubled and violent characters who consistently violate policy and law to bring criminals to justice or as almost super-human figures who are karate, CSI, and shooting experts able to solve complex crimes and vanquish violent criminals in less than an hour *sans* commercial interruptions.

Reality TV police shows such as *Cops* ultimately do police a disservice, because the involved officers are mesmerized and distracted by the camera; they over-react to get their 15 minutes of fame and more often than not act stupidly and recklessly on camera.

I use *Cops* episodes in training police officers in what *not* to do in the field. However, the uninformed viewer does not know the difference between real police work and reality TV – i.e., contrived fantasy police work. As a result, juries walk into the courtroom with a preconceived bias against police, or they experience what is referred to as the "CSI effect" – they have unrealistic expectations of what police can and cannot do.

The best service America's media can provide for this country and its law enforcement and criminal justice system is to *simply report the news accurately and fairly*. As all forensic experts and attorneys understand, every case "is what it is," with all of its positives, negatives and unknowns.

News reporters and commentators need to objectively investigate the circumstances, facts, and forensic evidence of every case they report on before airing the story. There simply is no excuse or justification not to. They need to know that it is OK to simply report brief circumstances and facts known and confirmed at the time, without speculation.

The public needs to know what you have *objectively learned,* not what you speculatively *believe* happened in a police-involved crime story. Simply tell your viewers or listeners that you don't know all the facts of a case at the time of reporting.

Finally, getting your news story out *right* is far more important to the community, law enforcement, and the criminal justice system than getting the story out *first*.

Chapter 11

The Black Lives Matter movement's 10-point policing program: a dose of reality is needed

The militant Black Lives Matter (BLM) movement currently fills up the air and print space of national and international news. They appear to be everywhere, staging protest marches, disrupting political candidates during rallies and speeches, waving signs and shouting their rage. BLM activist members even appear on Fox News and other national media outlets, spewing half-truths, misrepresentations, and outright lies about the fact patterns of violent police encounters with young black men.

Last year, presidential candidate Hillary Clinton met with Black Lives Matter activist leaders and encouraged them to develop a platform of the changes they would like to see in American policing. As a result, BLM movement leaders have developed a 10-point program for ending police shootings and alleged acts of brutality; they now refer to it as "Campaign Zero." Since the news media have only sporadically covered this plan, I am taking an opportunity to discuss it, along with my impressions of its viability.

Here's a hint. Very little of the BLM's 10-point program is rational or viable. Let's discuss the plan point-by-point. But first, a reminder: These people lie. Don't build your policing upon falsehoods and fabrications.

In order to attempt to understand the Black Lives Matter movement, you must first realize that the entire movement is founded upon a number of false narratives. Some of these I have already discussed in this book. For instance, in introducing the BLM's 10-point plan, BLM activist/supporter Molly Weasley of the blog politicalmurder.com erroneously writes that "More than 1,000 people are killed each year by police. Of those, nearly 60% were unarmed." However, Ms. Weasley fails to list where she pulled up that statistic.

That's because one doesn't exist. It's a blatant lie. That's what the BLM movement leaders and their surrogates do. They literally make stuff up! They simply don't tell the truth and hope that a naïve and uninformed American population doesn't do their homework to find out what the facts are.

Thus, as I have repeatedly emphasized, the key to understanding deadly confrontations involving police is to know the objective, scientific, and forensic facts.

First of all, the USDOJ statistics I have produced clearly show that police kill nowhere near the 1,000 a year that Ms. Beasley claims.

Next, let's look at Ms. Beasley's comment that "60% of subjects killed by police are allegedly unarmed" and consider it from a police standpoint. The FBI's *Law Enforcement Officers Killed & Assaulted* statistics document that in 2013 alone, 27 officers were killed by firearms. Of those, 26, or 96%, were killed by suspects using firearms.

Eighteen of the 26 officers (61.5%) were killed by suspects armed with handguns. During that same year, 434 (69%) of 626 federal officers assaulted by suspects, were assaulted by *armed* suspects. Of those, 198 were attacked by blunt instruments, 121 by vehicles, 88 by firearms, and 27 by suspects wielding edged weapons.

How do these vetted statistics reconcile with Ms. Beasley's claims that approximately 60% of suspects encountered by police in violent confrontations are "unarmed"? They don't.

Here's another one of those inconvenient truths that undermine the BLM mythology. According to the yearly FBI statistics of law enforcement officers killed in action, approximately 41% of officers killed by violent means are killed by *black males.* A review of the available statistics indicates that black males murder police officers at a rate nearly _8 times higher_ than the rate of black males who die during police use-of-force encounters. However, you never will hear anyone from the Black Lives Matter movement or the mainstream media mention this. *Why not?*

Now let's analyze the movement's 10-point plan to repair our law enforcement and justice system.

#1 – **End broken windows policing**.

The BLM demands an end to this time tested and proven policing strategy of patrol officers proactively enforcing minor/misdemeanor crimes. They especially want this enforcement curtailed in minority neighborhoods.

Minor crimes to them are violations such as prostitution, minor drug sales, drug influence, petty thefts, vandalism, and weapons possession.

Really? Are those the crimes you want the police to forget about in *your* neighborhood? Do you think that there might be a relationship between these misdemeanor crimes and more serious and violent crimes? Of course there is, and that is why in every community where the proactive "broken windows" or, in my time, a "shake, rattle and roll" enforcement strategy, has been applied, overall crime has been reduced. When that strategy is removed, crime rises again. New York City is an excellent example of this.

#2 – **Community oversight of law enforcement**.

This involves the use of civilians overseeing and monitoring police actions, including uses of force, such as a Police Commissioner and civilian review boards. Having worked on one as a consulting expert, I have no problem with this concept, as long as the members of the police commission or civilian review board are (1) properly vetted for background and biases; (2) not politically selected; and (3) more importantly, professionally trained in the law and police practices.

The problem is that while a number of large cities employ civilian review boards, relatively few are successful. This is because their members are politically selected, have biases against police, and lack the proper level of training needed to make forensic, rather than emotional or political decisions.

#3 – Limit the use of force.

This demand is intended to establish standards to monitor how force is used by police. We already have this; it's called "the law" and "department policies." "The law" means the 4th and 14th Amendments, as well as State and Federal statutes and Federal civil rights case laws – all provide legal criminal and civil standards or guidelines by which police actions and uses of force are evaluated and judged.

Police departments develop and implement administrative policies that are enforced through the disciplinary process. All States have commissions on peace officer standards, and the standards of police practices are codified in the officers' training. There are also national bodies that provide codified police standards.

In fact, no other criminal justice profession has more laws and standards than law enforcement, and rightly so. Also, the police internal affairs investigation system is consistently better and more professional and holds officers more accountable than the complaint mechanisms for police counterparts, such as state attorney bar associations, commissions on judicial review for judges, and inspector general offices that monitor and punish government abuse of authority and corruption.

Anyone taking the time to research statistics on police discipline, versus the discipline, sanctions, expulsions, and prison terms meted out to corrupt attorneys, judges, and politicians, will quickly find that far more police officers are disciplined, terminated from employment, and/or sent to jail/prison than any of their criminal or civil justice counterparts - or politicians.

What is missing in the BLM's demand regarding limiting police uses of force is specifically what techniques, tactics and/or weaponry they are suggesting be limited or removed. That's very important to know. Without knowing this, their demand to "limit the use of force" is far from viable.

#4 – Independently investigate and prosecute police for alleged violations.

As the director of a team of professional investigators, medical personnel, and applied scientists who are trained and experienced in independently reviewing officer-involved shootings, in-custody deaths and other uses of force, I am in favor of this.

Even though I find that in the majority of cases, law enforcement generally does a credible job of investigating uses of force, I find that even at the Federal and State level, detectives' investigative and applied science skills can be lacking. I also find that major investigations can be hampered by budgets, manpower constraints, the lack of forensic equipment, and the occasional occupational bias.

I favor an independent, multidisciplinary approach to the investigation of serious police uses of force. But given that officers are already prosecuted, punished, and imprisoned far more than guilty attorneys or politicians, it's hard to know what "more" must be done.

#5 – Community representation.

Again, I am in favor of this. It is also important to know that for several decades, police departments have done nearly everything possible to recruit, select, and train suitable minority candidates to become law enforcement officers. However, this has become a most difficult task, not because of racism, as has been suggested by the BLM movement, but rather because candidates from *all* communities we see often lack the appropriate education, social skills, mindset, and physical skills needed for this unique and demanding job.

It is important for you to understand that many applicants for law enforcement positions cannot pass a background check. As an example, in early 2016 the Los Angeles County Sheriff's Department reported that only two out of 100 applicants for the position of Deputy Sheriff passed their multiphasic and background examinations, in order to be accepted into the sheriff's academy.

Just to put this into perspective, I can guarantee you that neither President Obama nor former Secretary of State Hillary Clinton could pass even the most basic background investigation to become a police officer. As a former Police Academy director and a field training officer, I can attest that the wash-out rate in the Police Academy and in the Field Training Program is significant.

The "Ferguson Effect"

In a recent article "Police Department's Nationwide Struggling to Find New Recruits," published by PoliceMag.com, police expert James Chriss, who has authored a book on community policing, has identified what some experts in the law enforcement community are referring to as "The Ferguson Effect" as a major reason why people are now shying away from law enforcement as a career. Chriss states that the "heightened media sensationalism over police use of force is probably scaring away a lot of people." [33]

In my almost daily contacts with the law enforcement community, I hear a theme that "The Job" of police work and community service is no longer resonating with career officers. They tell me that the pay is too low and the personal and professional risks to them are too great. Many police officers do not feel that the community appreciates the work they do, the sacrifices they make, and the extreme risks they take on the public's behalf. This is a true shame and a serious problem that America may take a long time to recover from, if indeed we ever recover from this tragedy. This new police mindset is most certainly an unfortunate consequence of this new "War on Police."

The BLM movement, the media, and the general public all need to understand that when you appropriately demand that police be properly selected and well trained, you naturally restrict the selection process. You can't have it both ways. You also don't want biased,

---

[33] www.policemag.com/channel/careers-training/news/2016/03/07

emotionally persuaded officers who base their actions upon speculation rather than objective or forensic facts when they make decisions about detentions, arrests, searches and seizures.

More importantly, you do *not* want underqualified, armed police officers on the street making split-second decisions involving detentions, arrests, vehicle pursuits, and uses of force, including deadly force.

In real police life, there are no "do-overs."

Have you ever watched those videos posted by various police departments who have invited complaining, accusatory community activists or reporters to come in to play "police officer for a day" and then videotaped how they respond to difficult and challenging role playing scenarios with officers playing the role of suspicious or resistant suspects?

These videos are an education for the activist or reporter, because in almost all of the taped scenarios I have watched or participated in as a role player, the "officer" usually uses unnecessary, excessive force - or shoots and kills the unarmed role-player "suspect" who poses no imminent threat that would justify such a use of force. These activists and reporters quickly learn that being a police officer is a very difficult, mentally demanding, and challenging job. They also learn that circumstances and life can change in a millisecond.

In the training environment, you can make a mistake and get a "do-over." However, in real life there are no "do-overs;" there is only life and death.

#6 – Body cameras and filming the police in action.

This point would require that police officers and their vehicles be integrated with video devices. Again, I am generally in favor of this. However, there are several implementation problems that need to be overcome and understood. First, it is very costly and the majority of police departments would not be able to afford it. Federal grants would go far to make this happen.

Next, the public needs to understand that scientifically, video cameras don't always depict the "totality of circumstances" that is critical in the ultimate analysis of a police action or use of force. The camera shows only what it is pointed at, and we live in a 360° world. Departments also have to implement reasonable policies on the use of body cameras so that officer safety is not affected.

Next, the BLM movement wants to ensure that citizens have the right to record police interactions. They already have this right. It's called the 1st Amendment. However, what is needed is better police training that reminds officers that citizens have this right. And citizens also need to be reminded that once a person records a police encounter, that recording automatically becomes forensic evidence. Police have the right to collect and review evidence, but not to confiscate a citizen's camera or cell phone. Again, mutual training is needed so that the delicate balance of evidence collection and civil rights is maintained.

#7 – Better police training.

Few police administrators, trainers and officers will argue with this point. We are always clamoring for more and better training. The BLM movement wants more training on "racial bias." Police officers receive plenty of this training at the Police Academy. I would suggest that *the people who really need to receive better training are private citizens and the news media.* I would make this training mandatory. In my opinion, citizens, beginning at the elementary school level, should receive training on their civil rights, the law, and the job and legal authority of police officers.

Members of the news media covering and reporting on police actions should receive mandated training on these issues and police bias as well. I say this because every day, reporters demonstrate a definite lack of knowledge of police practices, police legal authority, and civil rights when they report on police investigations and uses of force. As long as the BLM movement recognizes that education and training is a two-way street, I support this point.

#8 – <u>Ending "for profit" policing</u>.

The movement wants "an end to quota systems and limits on fines for low-income people." As a retired police officer, I would agree that quota systems are bad. They still exist in some areas and should be permanently removed. When municipalities covertly adopt "write a lot of tickets" programs to increase city coffers as an informal "tax," they inadvertently place a wedge between members of their community and their police force. This mentality needs to end.

However, it is important to understand that the courts and municipalities set the bail schedules for fines. It would appear unconstitutional and unduly discriminatory to give preferential treatment to low-income offenders over those who earn more. Therefore, this is not a viable solution. Here's a better one that is guaranteed to both reduce the crime rate while allowing low-income offenders to keep more money in their pockets. *Stop committing crimes!* It's just that simple.

#9 – <u>End the "militarization" of the police</u>.

This point seeks to end the Federal government's 1033 Program that provides military-grade weapons to local police departments. I think BLM movement supporters need to first identify what types of military-grade weapons they do not want their police to have. Then we can have a reasonable discussion.

It is important to know that President Obama, who has generally been an advocate of the Black Lives Matter movement, recently issued an Executive Order to dissolve the 1033 Program. Soon after the President signed this order, which effectively takes military Bearcat-type armored protection vehicles away from police, we experienced terrorist attacks in Paris, France and San Bernardino, CA. In these instances, if the French and California officers responding had lost the use of these life-saving vehicles, many more officers and civilians no doubt would have been killed by heavily armed terrorists.

There are some items of military equipment that enhance police and community safety. There are admittedly others that are frivolous and not needed. Let's identify each. This will not be difficult to do.

#10 – Have "fair" police contracts.

The BLM movement believes that union labor contracts offer police officers too much protection in instances of misconduct. Supporters call for the elimination of barriers that prevent the public from reviewing an officer's disciplinary history. In addition, they call for an end to paying officers while they are on administrative leave while being investigated for an alleged use of excessive force.

Obviously, there are many obstructions to the viability of this final point. They are referred to as "labor laws," an officer's "civil rights" and "due process."

Let me get this right. BLM movement activists march against police alleged abuses of civil rights - yet they have no problem with taking away some of those same protections for police officers? They want police officers immediately suspended without pay before they have been found guilty of alleged violations? These activists who so vehemently protest police alleged violations of due process in deadly force confrontations want to violate that same due process for an officer being investigated? Does anyone see a problem here?

Next, regarding the public's "need to know," versus its "right to know" about an accused officer's personnel files: these files are protected by labor and other civil laws. There are firm criminal and civil remedies already in place to ensure that this balance is maintained. The trier of fact in any determination as to whether or not an accused officer's personnel file can be opened to the public is the court. There are no problems with this system, and I agree with it.

In summary, much of the 10-point "Campaign Zero" program of the Black Lives Matter movement lacks substance and viability because the demands are

- not feasible (as with the conflict between more minority hires and police effectiveness);
- illicit (denying officers due process);
- not completely effective (the limitations of body cams);
- unrealistic or unproductive (police should ignore weapons possession, prostitution, and vandalism?);
- prohibitively costly (the cost of body cams);
- or lacking in factual context to support the desired changes (exactly what "military" equipment should police not have?).

To date, the leaders and activists of the BLM movement have been unwilling to listen to, or even research reliable objective facts when those facts are plainly out there. *Until the movement's leaders and supporters are willing to honestly look at the socio-criminal and political issues that underlie high crime rates - and the disinformation that drives this new War on Police that they in part have instigated - they can never be taken seriously.*

References

"Examining the Prevalence of Death from Police Use of Force," Johnson, Richard, Ph.D., © 2015, University of Toledo

U.S. Dept. of Justice, FBI Uniform Crime Report Supplemental Homicide Reports and U.S. Center for Disease Control death classifications, Jan. 2009 – Jan. 2012

National Safety Council, *Injury Facts* (2012), www.nsc.org

www.cdc.gov/violenceprevention/suicide/statistics/aag.html

https://www.fbi.gov/about-us/cjis/ucr/leoka/2013/officers-feloniously-killed/felonious_topic_page_-2013

Molly, http://politicalmurder.com, 08-21-15

"Black Lives Matter activists outline policy goals," BBC News, 08-21-15, http://www.bbc.com/news/world-us-canada-34023751

"Black Lives Matter has a plan to radically change America's police," Speiser, Matthew, 08-24-15, http://www.businessinsider.com/Black-lives-matter-has-a-policy-platform-2015-8

"Police Disproportionately Killing Black Men – A False Narrative," Martinelli, Ron, Ph.D., 06-22-15, www.DrRonMartinelli.com, POLICEone.com

Summary: A few final thoughts

As a professional who has been actively engaged in law enforcement, criminal science, and forensics for over forty years, I can attest that I have never seen the relationship between law enforcement and the minority community so polarized and contentious since I began my career as a patrol officer. As a matter of fact, during a recent television debate between Democratic Presidential candidates Hillary Clinton and Bernie Sanders, a black CNN moderator began his question on race relations by offering that relationships between blacks, whites and law enforcement have been deteriorating over the past ten years. As I've said, I don't disagree, but as a criminologist and a political spectator, I also know the reasons for that.

For those who are of older generations, one would think that we were living in the days of the civil rights abuses and demonstrations of the 1950s–1960s: massive protest marches, "Negroes" being assaulted with fire hoses and vicious police dogs and beaten with long batons. Racial oppression was a cancer on our body politic.

While those horrors are factually much different from today's typical encounters between the minority and law enforcement communities, you would never know it if you listened to the leaders and supporters of the Black Lives Matter movement, the race-baiting activists like Jesse Jackson and Al Sharpton, and pandering politicians like President Obama, Eric Holder, Hillary Clinton, and Bernie Sanders, forever attempting to enhance their voter appeal.

When people are solely fixated on the issue of race, they tend to view everything that happens to themselves and others of their racial group through a prism that only has two colors – black (oppressed) and white (oppressors). That is far from the reality in America today. It is a biased, self-serving perception and a falsehood, because this is not the 1950s or the 1960s. Blacks and other minorities have made and continue to make significant strides in every facet of American life: education, the sciences, employment, the military, political leadership, economics, the arts, the entertainment industry, and sports, just to name a few.

In what other nation or culture where a black minority population that comprises a mere 13% of the population would you find that country's President, as leader of the free world, and a number of members of this nation's executive cabinet, as well as high ranking political officials coming from that same population, and in such a relatively short time span? Nowhere else but America, the land of infinite opportunity for advancement, no matter what your race, religion or culture is.

This is why people risk their lives to come here to live, rather than immigrate (or sneak) into China, North Korea, Cuba, Russia, Eastern Europe, or some nations in Africa and the Middle East - places that have *real* oppression and "state-sponsored violence."

The Black Lives Matter movement treats the black, media, American, and international communities as mushroom farmers handle their crop – they keep everyone in the darkness by using denial, deflection and redirection, while feeding Marxist manure/propaganda to the masses.

If one pays close attention to the rhetoric of the BLM movement, its supportive activists, and their political surrogates, you hear the same tired language of those current and past radical, nationalist political regimes that have truly oppressed other people: the "liberation of oppressed people," "state sponsored violence," "rise up and fight oppression," and so on.

If you were a history buff like me, you would recognize literally all of the slogans of the leaders and supporters of the Black Lives Matter movement as identical to those previously voiced by violent revolutionaries and tyrannical leaders of the past like Adolph Hitler, Benito Mussolini, Vladimir Lenin, Josef Stalin, Mao Tse-tung, Fidel Castro, and Che Guevara.

Unfortunately, BLM movement supporters of the Millennium Generation have little to no idea who those monsters were, or how they really segregated, oppressed, and murdered entire segments of their populations to assume and hold on to power. The young, undereducated and uninformed simply have no historical context to draw from, and the leaders of the BLM movement depend on that to forward their message of false narratives, separatism and hate.

Black Lives Matter movement co-founders Alicia Garza, Patrisse Cullors, and Opal Tometi, and other BLM leaders freely admit their allegiance to and belief in the Marxist ideology of a number of the radical and violent Black Nationalist revolutionaries of our nation's recent past. BLM leaders openly state that their role models are people like cop-killer and former Black Panther Party and Black Liberation Army militant Assata Shakur, former Black Panther leaders Angela Davis, killer George Jackson, Huey Newton and others. In fact, some BLM members, during BLM demonstrations, even wear T-shirts with the likenesses of these criminals.

The leaders and supporters of the BLM movement follow the teachings of black separatism, Black Nationalism, the Black Liberation Army, and the Weather Underground of the violent era of the 1960s and 1970s. The goals, objectives and designs of the Black Lives Matter movement are to resurrect the far-leftist, militant, and revolutionary atmosphere of our past, but with a more educated, sophisticated, better organized, well-funded, and politically and social-media savvy organization.

The ultimate designs of the BLM movement are clearly to exploit and exacerbate tensions between the black and law enforcement communities and to diminish, defund, and eventually dissolve law enforcement so that they can begin the process of degrading our nation's rule of law.

There is no ambiguity about the designs of the BLM movement. They are engaged in a very sophisticated war on America's police and criminal justice system. This is known as "asymmetrical warfare," and America's law enforcement, criminal justice, political, and black communities had better wake up quickly and recognize this problem before it gets further out of control.

The Black Lives Matter movement preaches and consistently seeks to implement the rhetoric of hate. If there is one thing we don't need in this country, it is yet another "outsider" militant political group preaching hate and advocating for violence against law enforcement. When you march down city streets wearing T-shirts and carrying banners that say, "Black Lives Matter," while yelling hateful and violent rhetoric like *"Pigs in a blanket. Fry 'em like bacon!"* it's hard to disavow that you are not a violent, hateful, and anti-law enforcement group and claim that what you really want is peace.

The great irony of the Black Lives Matter movement is that while the leaders, supporters and political surrogates of the movement and others like MORE, MoveOn.org, Occupy and others block freeways and streets and disrupt political rallies, while chanting rhetoric about various politicians and "The State" oppressing the civil rights and freedoms of "the people;" this is exactly what *they* themselves are doing. This is not simply an irony, but the specific intent of this movement. These radical, leftist, disruptive and occasionally violent political groups demonstrate that they are the *real* oppressors of civil rights and free speech; not those whom they protest against.

As you watch the BLM movement demonstrations on television and listen to the extremist rhetoric of its leaders and supporters, pause to consider what other peaceful political party or group advocates for violence against and the murder of police officers, *"Pigs in a blanket. Fry 'em like bacon?"* *"What do we want? Dead cops. When do we want them? Now!"* What other peaceful political groups or organizations disrupt political rallies to squelch the right of free speech of political candidates? What other peaceful political groups or organizations have members and supporters who engage in rioting, looting and burning down businesses in some of the poorest minority communities in our nation?

After you have considered this, I ask you to tell me who are the *real* oppressors of civil rights and free speech in this country? Who are the *real* purveyors of disruption, revolution and violence – the police, or the members of the Black Lives Matter movement, their supporters and surrogates, who not only engage in such activity, but do nothing to disavow those who do? Therein lies your answer.

Can law enforcement and government work with the Black Lives Matter movement in an effort to assuage the black community?

Succinctly, no. First, it is important to understand that contrary to all of the BLM movement's propaganda and the uninformed mainstream media's attention to their cause, *the BLM movement does not represent the vast majority of black Americans or other people of color*. They are outsiders demanding entry into the house of racial solidarity and cooperation that so many Americans of all colors have worked so hard to build - and then threatening to burn the house down if their demands are not met.

That is not the way negotiations are held and progress is achieved. The BLM movement's clamoring, threats, and acts of overt violence against law enforcement and local government, as we see on the 24/7 "Breaking News" cycle, are attempts at extortion that should never be paid.

Next, although the Black Lives Matter movement tells us that they are speaking for and working on behalf of the black community, their historic actions do not reconcile with their rhetoric. One has only to look at all the black-owned and patronized businesses being systematically looted and burned in cities like Ferguson and Baltimore.

No, the co-founders and leaders of the BLM movement are seeking political power that they can eventually leverage in their Marxist war against law enforcement, the criminal justice system, and local government, to ultimately overthrow the rule of law and create their own idealistic form of a black separatist government founded upon Marxist ideology. Again, it is not hard to discover what the BLM co-founders and movement is all about, and this book provides you with all the reference materials you need.

How should the Black Lives Matter movement be addressed?

First of all, because of the extreme risks the Black Lives Matter movement poses to the safety and security of this nation, it is my opinion that if the organization, its co-founders, and its leaders and followers incite and/or participate in violent, destructive acts, then government, the criminal justice system, and law enforcement should do everything in their power to dissolve it.

However, the problem of dissolving the Black Lives Matter movement cannot be addressed by law enforcement, or local, state, and Federal governments alone. In my opinion, *the most important people who need to be involved in disbanding the movement are blacks themselves.*

Clearly, the black community needs to disavow this militant, dangerous and destructive radical organization in the same way that Middle Easterners should disavow ISIL, ISIS, Hamas, or any other destructive group.

First and foremost, the black community, law enforcement, political leaders, and the mainstream media all need to inform themselves about what the Black Lives Matter organization is all about, who their leaders are, what political ideologies they believe in, who their role models are, and what the goals, objectives, and designs of the organization are. This book acts a guidebook for doing just that. It's a first step in proactively marginalizing the BLM movement and minimizing its destructive effects.

Next, and equally important, we must address the black community's valid concerns about the nature of some of the contacts that police have with its members. Government and the criminal justice and law enforcement communities must recognize the special needs and problems of the black community and people of color and continue to work with these communities to end the polarization and build bridges of understanding based upon real issues, rather than false and divisive narratives.

The black community also needs to be honest with itself about the historic problems that have precluded many in their communities from moving forward in their lives: teen pregnancy; father abandonment, single-mother households, and the breakdown of the family unit; child neglect and abuse; high secondary-education dropout rates; a failure to value continuing education and obtaining real job skills; moving away from religious faith; joining and maintaining a street gang lifestyle; drug and alcohol abuse; selling drugs; disproportional criminal recidivism; the glorification of hip-hop and gangster rap music and videos which glorify drug sales, gangs, violence and the sexual exploitation of young women; and gun violence. All of this results in the institutionalized, disproportionate incarceration and imprisonment of young black men and women.

The black community and the media need to do a much better job at vetting individuals whom they then advertise and forward to the black community as being "black community leaders." When race baiters, race-card extortionists and spreaders of false narratives like the Revs. Jesse Jackson and Al Sharpton; the latter being a well-known tax evader, are presented as "black leaders," this is troubling.

When Rev. Al Sharpton extorts a black audience at Stephen Marks Kean College (NJ) in 1992 to murder whites and police officers in screaming to his assembly, *"I'll off the man. Well, off him. Plenty of crackers walking around here tonite!"* and *"I believe in offing the pigs. Well they got pigs out here."* This violent rhetoric does not move the black community forward in their relationships with whites or with law enforcement. In fact, it is not only hate speech, but domestic terrorist hate speech that some legal analysts might argue was not an expression of free speech, but a crime.[34]

It is both interesting and disappointing to note that White House records document that from 2009 to March 20, 2016, Al Sharpton has been invited to and has visited the White House a total of sixty-one times. Name any other American citizen who has both threatened and publically extorted other American citizens to kill white people and

---

[34] https://www.youtube.com/watch?v=IXeHzXakS_Q

police officers, who has been a repeated guest of our President in the "People's House?" I hope that you get my point regarding where the current administration's support lies with respect to our law enforcement and non-minority communities. This record is as much extremely troubling, as it is racially polarizing. This is not the type of hope and "fundamental change" in America that we were promised seven years ago when this President took office. If you think about it, we are moving backwards as a nation towards increasing divisions between race and the law enforcement community that were certainly not present to this extent under previous Republican and Democratic administrations. In short, we have indeed experienced change in our country and in our American society – but little of it has been good for any of us. That is obvious.

It's a long and formidable list, and the black community must voice its extreme displeasure with these problems and commit itself to resolving the issues that have imprisoned them as hostages in their own communities. They can no longer afford to be "black holocaust" deniers of the horrendous statistics of black-on-black crime and homicides I have discussed in this book. The problems are real and getting worse every year.

Government, law enforcement, and the criminal justice system are not the panacea for overcoming the problems in those black and other minority communities that are blighted and depressed because of all the socio-cultural dysfunction and pathology. In fact, history shows that some small factions of the black community and those who seek to exploit that community, like the BLM movement, actually resent government, law enforcement, and the criminal justice system for being involved as "outsiders." In truth, "outsiders" can do only so much. The reality will not change and will become progressively worse unless the good and law-abiding members of the black community finally say, *"Enough is enough!"*

Moreover, as I mentioned earlier, the mainstream media and politicians need to seriously take the time to educate themselves about who and what the Black Lives Matter movement is all about. Rather than seeking the support of the BLM movement to leverage self-serving voter turnout and photo-ops, they need to disavow the movement and instead work with the law abiding and respected members of the black community, educators, and clergy to effect positive change.

Investigative reporters need to use their skills to peel back the curtain of deceit, false narratives and Marxist propaganda - and write objective, factually based stories about police-involved shootings, in-custody deaths, and other high-profile incidents. News commentators need to ask BLM co-founders, leaders, surrogates, and supporters tough, probative questions that confront the movement's false narratives and shed light on its real goals, objectives and political designs.

Law-abiding Americans who are supportive of law enforcement, as well as those who comprise the law enforcement, forensic, and religious communities, should publically disavow all of those business persons, politicians, activists, and celebrities who support and provide funding to the Black Lives Matter movement. They should also boycott the businesses, products, movies, music, concerts, and promotional products owned, produced, and advertised by these individuals.

If a celebrity who supports the BLM movement is publicizing his/her work on television or radio, those who oppose the movement and its actions should call, write, or email and threaten to boycott any media outlet that accepts money for advertising those celebrities' music, movies, or other entertainment products.

Ultimately, celebrities are controlled when they are sanctioned economically. They are hypocritical, shallow and fickle. Once they see that their income has been reduced or redacted, their rhetoric and misplaced advocacy stops. Hypocritical celebrity supporters and surrogates of the Black Lives Matter movement need to be "outed" not only for their "under the radar" financial support for the BLM movement, but for their hypocrisy in their deliberate ignorance of the oppression of national and international human rights by those oppressors they support and economically profit from.

Further, no on-duty, off-duty, or retired law enforcement officer should accept any on-duty or paid employment to provide security for any person or celebrity who actively or covertly supports or funds the BLM movement through business interests or celebrity engagements.

Those current or retired officers who accept voluntary, paid security assignments from celebrities who in any way support or fund the Black Lives Matter movement are simply not worthy of the badge of authority they wear or have worn.

No controversial celebrity can afford public appearances without police providing security. When police group together with a unified mission not to provide celebrities like Jay Z and Beyoncé with protection, these anti-police personalities will curtail many of their major public appearances. Hence, another drastic drop in their personal income. When money – or the lack of it talks – "BS" walks. It's just that simple.

Finally, everyone needs to recognize and remain focused on and committed to the theme that we are *all* Americans and not hyphenated, separate cultures that need to be differentiated and separated from each other. We share a unique land of opportunity, not paralleled or copied, much less equaled, by any other nation on this earth.

As a nation of mixed races and cultures, we share a symbiotic relationship as Americans. We are currently engaged in a dynamic struggle for the very soul of our nation's core values. We can stand by and do nothing while purveyors of hate and racial dissention forward anti-police, anti-government false narratives in an attempt to usurp the rule of law and our Democratic way of life. Or, we can stand up, lean forward and dismantle these Marxists and anarchists who are intent upon oppressing the freedoms and solidarity of our still proud nation to further their own revolutionary designs.

We all need to work together to unite our nation and move it forward......because the simple fact is that - a*ll lives matter.*

Ron L. Martinelli, Ph.D., CMI-V

March, 2016

Bibliography

Control, U. C. (2016, 1 30). *FBI Uniform Crime Report Supplemental Homicide Reports, Jan 2009-Jan 2012.* Retrieved 01 21, 2016, from www.cdc.gov.

David, K. R. (2012). *Use of Force Investigation.* Bloomington: Responder Media.

DiMaio, V. J. (1999). *Gunshot Wounds, 2nd Edition.* Boca Raton: CRC Press.

Garrison, D. H. (2003). *Practical Shooting Scene Investigation: The Investigation and Reconstruction of Crime Scenes Invovling Gunfire.* Boca Raton: Universal Publishers.

Grossman, D. C. (1996). *On Killing, The Psychological Cost of Learning to Kill in War and Society.* New York: Back Bay Books.

Haag, L. (2006). *Shooting Incident Reconstruction.* San Diego: Academic Press.

Hatch, D. E. (2003). *Officer-Involved Shootings and Use of Force.* New York: CRC Press.

Janell Ross, R. (2015, 10 25). Black Lives Matter Launches a Polictical Action Committee. But it's Not an Easy Fit. *Washington Post.*

Johnston, R. P. (2015). *Examining the Prevalence of Death from Police Use of Force.* Univesity of Toledo.

Martinelli, R. P. (2011, 02). Pre-contact Threat Assessment and the "Art of Force". *Peace Officers Research Association of California News*, pp. 30-32.

Muhammad, C. (2015, 09 30). Tensions Mount at LAPD Public Meeting. *National News Reporter.*

Patrick, U. W. (2010). *In Defense of Self and Others: Issues, Facts & Fallacies - The Realities of Law Enforcements Use of Deadly Force.* Durham: Carolina Academic Press.

Sealov, M. (n.d.). Interview of Patrisse Cullors. *Vice UK.*

Sharp, M. J. (2008, 10 22). To Shoot or Not to Shoot: Response and Interpretation of Response to Armed Assailant. *The Forensic Examiner.*

Sharps, M. P. (2010). *Processing Under Pressure: Stress, Memory and Decison Making in Law Enforcement.* Flushing: Loose Leaf Publishing.

Vilos, J. D. (2013). *Self-Defense Laws of All 50 States.* Centerville: Guns West Publishing.

REFERENCES

Legal Cites

Graham v. Connor, 490 U.S. 386, 396-97, 109 S.Ct. 1865, 1872, 104 L.Ed.2d 443 (1989) – Use of Force

Saucier v. Katz, 533 U.S. 194, 201 (2001) – Use of Force

Forrester v. City of San Diego, 25 F.3d 804 (9th Cir. 1994) – Use of Force

Tennessee v. Garner, 471 U.S. 1 (1985) – Use of Force/Warnings/Deadly Force

Garnett v. Athens-Clarke County, 378 F.3d 1274, 1280, n. 12 (11th Cir. 2004) – Use of Force

Forrett v. Richardson, 112 F.3d 416 (9th Cir. 1997) – Use of Force

Deering v. Reich, 183 F.3d 645, 652-53 (7th Cir. 1999) – Use of Force

Collins v. Nagle, 892 F.2d 489, 493 (6th Cir. 1989) – Use of Force

Sokolaw (1989) 490 U.S. 1, 7-8 – Tony C. (1978) 21 Cal. 3d 888, 893 – Detention

Twilley (9th Cir. 2000) 222 F. 3d 1092, 1095 – Detention

Andre P., (1991) 226 Cal. App. 3d 1164, 1169 – Detention

Hodari D. (1991) 499 U.S. 621, 627-628 – Detention

Wardlow (2000) 528 U.S. 119 – Reasonable Suspicion/Detention

White (1990) 496 U.S. 325, 330 – Reasonable Suspicion/Detention

Mims (1992) 9 Cal.App 4th 1244, 1248 – Special Knowledge/Detain

Hensley (1985) 469 U.S. 221 – Detention – Knowledge from Others

State Statutes

FL Statute Title XLVI, Ch. 776, §§776.012(1); 776.013

FL S.A. §776.012 – Use of Force in Defense of Person; No Duty to Retreat

FL S.A. §776.08 – Forcible Felony

FL S.A. §784.011 – Assault

FL S.A. §784.021 – Aggravated Assault

FL S.A. §784.045 – Aggravated Battery

FL S.A. §776.06 – Deadly Force

FL S.A. §782.04 – Murder

FL S.A. §782.07 – Manslaughter

Website References

www.BlackDemographics.com

www.linkedin.com/profile/AliciaGarza

www.en.wikipedia.org/wiki/Assata_Shakur

www.huffingtonpost.com/2013/10/01/jay-z-drug-dealer_n_4019023.html

www.facebook.com/pages/patrisse-cullors

www.ellabakercenter.org/about/staff-and-board/partisse-cullors

www.politico.com/magazine/politico50/2015/alicia-garza-patrisse-cullors-opal-tometi

www.web.calstatela.edu/academic/pas/Abdullah.ph.p

www.en.wikipedia.org/wiki/jay_Z

www.opensocietyfoundations.org/people/george-soros

www.humanevents.com/2011/04/02/top-10-reasons-george-soros-is-dangerous/

www.opensecrets.org/news/2010/09/opensecrets-battle-koch-brothers/

www.discoverthenetworks.org/funderProfile.asp?fndid=5184

www.theblaze.com/stories/2012/06/04/special-report-george-soros-godfather-of-the-left/

www.discoverthenetworks.org/viewSubCategory.asp?id=589

www.washingtontimes.com/news/2015/jan/14/george-soros-funds-ferguson-protests-hopes-to-spur/?page=all

www.vibe.com/2015/05/jay-z-Beyoncè-money-protesters-baltimore-ferguson/

www.theguardian.com/lifeandstyle/lostinshowbiz/2010/jan/08/Beyonc è-colonel-gaddafi-son

www.mediaite.com/online/confirmed-Beyoncè-sings-for-gaddafis-son-on-new-years/

www.telegraph.co.uk/news/worldnews/northamerica/usa/8371731/Div as-and-despots-the-stars-who-sing-for-dictators.html

www.mediaite.com/online/Beyoncè-new-years-eve-performing-for-gaddafi-family/

www.policemag.com/channel/patrol/news/2015/10/27/black-lives-matter-forms-political-action-committee.aspx

www.theblaze.com/stories/2015/10/20/black-lives-matter-protestors-rush-a-mayors-podium-at-town-hall-watch-what-happens-as-hes-escorted-out-for-safety/

www.domesticworkers.org

www.cjjc.org/

www.linkedin.com/profile/AliciaGarza

www.web.calstatela.edu/academic/pas/Abdullah.ph.p

www.socialistworker.org/2003-2/474/474_09_EllaBaker.shtml

www.dignityandpowernow.org

www.prisonerswithchildren.org/our-projects/allofus-or-none/

www.theblaze.com/stories/2015/10/20/black-lives-matter-protestors-rush-a-mayors-podium-at-town-hall-watch-what-happens-as-hes-escorted-out-for-safety/

www.finalcall.com/artman/publish/National_News2/article_102631.sht ml

National Safety Council, Injury Facts (2012), www.nsc.org

www.cdc.gov/violenceprevention/suicide/statistics/aag.html

www.usatoday.com/weather/resources/basics/wlighting.htm

www.drronmartinelli.com/2015/06/22/police-officers-disproportionally-killing black-men-another-false-narrative/

www.drronmartinelli.com/2015/09/05/black-lies-matter-the-forensic-facts-behind-the-false-narratives-of-this-violent-anti-police-movement/

www.mxgm.org/operation-ghetto-storm-2012-annual-report-on-the-extrajudicial-killing-of-313-black-people/

Safety Council, Injury Facts (2012), www.nsc.org

www.cdc.gov/violenceprevention/suicide/statistics/aag.html

www.usatoday.com/weather/resources/basics/wlighting.htm

www.drronmartinelli.com/2015/06/22/police-officers-disproportionally-killing-black-men-another-false-narrative/

www.drronmartinelli.com/2015/09/05/black-lies-matter-the-forensic-facts-behind-the-false-narratives-of-this-violent-anti-police-movement/

www.mxgm.org/operation-ghetto-storm-2012-annual-report-on-the-extrajudicial-killing-of-313-black-people/

www.BlackDemographics.com

www.en.wikipedia.org/wiki/Vietnam_War_casualties

www.en.wikipedia.org/wiki/United_States_military_casualties_of_war

"An unarmed black person is shot 'every 28 hours' says Marc Lamont Hill;" Sanders, Katie, © 08-26-14, *After the Fact*

"The viral claim that a black person is killed by police 'every 28 hours'," Ye Hee Lee, Michelle, © 12-24-14, FactChecker.com

"1 Black Man is Killed Every 28 Hours by Police or Vigilantes: America is Perpetually at War with its Own People," Hudson, Adam, © 05-28-13, Alternet.org

National Safety Council, Injury Facts (2012), www.nsc.org

www.cdc.gov/violenceprevention/suicide/statistics/aag.html

www.fbi.gov/about-us/cjis/ucr/leoka/2013/officers-feloniously-killed/felonious_topic_page_-2013

"Black Lives Matter offers 10-point plan to curb police killings;," Weasley, Molly, www.politicalmurder.com, 08-21-15

"Black Lives Matter activists outline policy goals," BBC News, 08-21-15, http://www.bbc.com/news/world-us-canada-34023751

"Black Lives Matter has a plan to radically change America's police," Speiser, Matthew, 08-24-15, http://www.businessinsider.com/black-lives-matter-has-a-policy-platform-2015-8

"Police Disproportionately Killing Black Men – A False Narrative"; Martinelli, Ron, Ph.D., 06-22-15, www.DrRonMartinelli.com, POLICEone.com

www.Blacklivesmatter.com

www.en.wikipedia.org/wiki/San_Quentin_Six

www.en.wikipedia.org/wiki/George_Jackson_(Black_Panther)

www.sfbayview.com/2013/07/the-revision-and-origin-of-black-august/

www.en.wikipedia.org/wiki/Fred_Hampton

"FBI Statistics: Officers Killed in the Line of Duty, 2012," *FBI Bulletin*, 05-13-13, www.fbi.gov/news/pressrel/press-releases/fbi-releases-2012-preliminary-statistics-for-law-enforcement-officers-killed-in-the-line-of-duty

"FBI Statistics: Officers Killed in the Line of Duty, 2011", FBI Bulletin, 05-14-12, www.fbi.gov/news/pressrel/press-releases/fbi-releases-2011-preliminary-statistics-for-law-enforcement-officers-killed-in-the-line-of-duty

"FBI Statistics: Officers Killed in the Line of Duty, 2010," *FBI Bulletin*, 05-10-11, www.fbi.gov/about-us/cjis/ucr/leoka/leoka-2010/officers-feloniously-killed

"Law Enforcement Officer Deaths – Mid-Year Report, 2012," Research Bulletin, National Law Enforcement Officers Memorial, www.nleomf.org/assets/pdfs/reports/valor/2012-Mid-Year-VALOR-Report.pdf

http://www.bls.gov/iif/oshwc/cfoi/jeh5_05_45-50.pdf

https://www.youtube.com/watch?v=lXeHzXakS_Q

http://www.freerepublic.com/focus/f-news/1816884/posts

http://www.newsmax.com/Newsfront/sharpton-fines-racism-taxes/2014/12/09/id/612015/

http://www.newsmax.com/Newsfront/sharpton-white-house-visits-Obamas/2014/12/12/id/612689/

https://www.whitehouse.gov/briefing-room/disclosures/visitor-records

Michael Brown Shooting

USDOJ Investigation Report Michael Brown OIS Incident

http://www.justice.gov/sites/default/files/opa/press-releases/attachments/2015/03/04/doj_report_on_shooting_of_michael_brown_1.pdf

OIS Crime Scene Diagram
https://smallicollective.files.wordpress.com/2014/12/michael_brown_shooting_scene_diagram-svg.png?w=1000&h=316

http://www.opposingviews.com/i/society/crime/report-darren-wilson-saved-black-babys-life-right-michael-browns-death

http://www.msnbc.com/msnbc/where-officer-darren-wilson-was-shooting-michael-brown

http://www.examiner.com/article/the-african-american-infant-darren-wilson-saved

Zimmerman Trial

Witness John Good's trial testimony

https://www.youtube.com/watch?v=i1fgmWEfSf4

https://en.wikipedia.org/wiki/Shooting_of_Trayvon_Martin#County_medical_examiner.27s_autopsy_report

Dr. Vincent DiMaio Zimmerman trial testimony

https://www.google.com/url?sa=t&rct=j&q=&esrc=s&source=web&cd=4&cad=rja&uact=8&ved=0CDMQtwlwA2oVChMII8DroJu5yAIVxosNCh0OcQn4&url=http%3A%2F%2Fwww.youtube.com%2Fwatch%3Fv%3DQ0FEVEqitY0&usg=AFQjCNFxHFV2WQuFfdPcU5UYSJkAAEqgpQ

http://www.usatoday.com/story/news/2015/02/24/no-federals-charges-against-george-zimmerman/23942297/

http://theconservativetreehouse.com/2015/05/28/controversial-florida-state-attorney-angela-corey-loses-counterclaim-suit-against-zimmerman-witness-ben-ruidbos/http://www.freerepublic.com/focus/news/3050299/posts